THE UNWRITTEN LAW OF CORPORATE REORGANIZATIONS

The law of corporate reorganizations controls the fate of enterprises worth billions of dollars and has reshaped entire sectors of the economy, yet its inner workings largely remain a mystery. Judges must police a small and closed fraternity of professionals as they sit down at a conference table and forge a new future for a distressed business, but little appears to tell judges how they are to do this. Judges, however, are in fact bound by a coherent set of unwritten principles that derive from a statute Parliament passed in 1571. These principles are not simply norms or customary practices. They have hard edges, judges must enforce them, and parties are bound by them as they are by any other law. This book traces the evolution of these unwritten principles and makes accessible a legal world that has long been closed off to outsiders.

Douglas G. Baird is Harry A. Bigelow Distinguished Service Professor of Law at the University of Chicago, and Chair of the National Bankruptcy Conference. A fellow of the American Academy of Arts and Sciences, he has served as a director and scholar-in-residence at the American College of Bankruptcy and is a past president of the American Law and Economics Association. His book *Elements of Bankruptcy* (7th edn., 2022) is regularly cited by the US Supreme Court and other appellate courts.

The Unwritten Law
of Corporate Reorganizations

Douglas G. Baird

University of Chicago

CAMBRIDGE
UNIVERSITY PRESS

University Printing House, Cambridge CB2 8BS, United Kingdom

One Liberty Plaza, 20th Floor, New York, NY 10006, USA

477 Williamstown Road, Port Melbourne, VIC 3207, Australia

314–321, 3rd Floor, Plot 3, Splendor Forum, Jasola District Centre, New Delhi – 110025, India

103 Penang Road, #05–06/07, Visioncrest Commercial, Singapore 238467

Cambridge University Press is part of the University of Cambridge.

It furthers the University's mission by disseminating knowledge in the pursuit of education, learning, and research at the highest international levels of excellence.

www.cambridge.org
Information on this title: www.cambridge.org/9781316512296
DOI: 10.1017/9781009058216

First published 2022

A catalogue record for this publication is available from the British Library.

ISBN 978-1-316-51229-6 Hardback
ISBN 978-1-009-06101-8 Paperback

For Julie and Sam

CONTENTS

PREFACE

The law of corporate reorganizations controls the fate of enterprises worth many billions of dollars and has reshaped entire sectors of the economy, yet its inner workings remain largely a mystery. Judges must police a small and closed fraternity of professionals as they sit down at a conference table and forge a new future for a distressed business, but little appears to tell judges how they are to do this.

The relevant statutes run to hundreds of pages and are rich with technical detail, but they say little about how the parties must conduct themselves during their negotiations. The few explicit statutory mandates are pitched at a high level of abstraction. They require little more than that the judge ensure that bargains be proposed in "good faith"[1] and be "fair and equitable."[2]

Precedent is similarly unhelpful. One can exhaust virtually all the guidance the Supreme Court has offered over the last century and a half in a few sentences: the judge cannot be a "silent registrar of agreements."[3] Nor can the judge approve deals that "alter the balance" of substantive rights set out in the statute.[4] At the same time, the judge should not come to the aid of a creditor who declines a "fair offer."[5] Lower courts are similarly silent. Among the many hundreds of

---

[1] 11 U.S.C. §1129(a)(3).

[2] 11 U.S.C. §1129(b)(1). To be sure, 11 U.S.C. §1129(b)(2) sets out what a plan needs in order to be "fair and equitable" as a substantive matter, but nothing is said about what it takes for the bargaining process itself to be "fair and equitable."

[3] See Louisville Trust Co. v. Louisville, New Albany & Chicago Railway Co., 174 U.S. 674, 688 (1899).

[4] See Czyzewski v. Jevic Holding Corp., 137 S. Ct. 973, 987 (2017).

[5] Northern Pacific Railway Co. v. Boyd, 228 U.S. 482, 508 (1913).

volumes of reported opinions, few provide much guidance about what
bargaining behavior is in bounds and what is out. Decided cases fail to
provide clear answers even for such basic questions as whether one
party can pay another to look the other way.[6]

Much less is up in the air than it first seems, however. The judge is
bound by a coherent set of unwritten principles that derive from
a statute Parliament passed in 1571. These principles are not simply
norms or customary practices. They have hard edges, judges must
enforce them, and parties are bound by them as they are by any other
law.

The Statute of 13 Elizabeth originally appeared merely to prohibit
a debtor from fraudulently conveying assets in order to defeat creditors,
but it was soon found to give judges the power to review any transaction
that undermined the rights of creditors. Over the course of the nineteenth century, judges drew on this power to craft an approach to
policing negotiations between creditors and a financially distressed
debtor. The legal reforms of the 1930s and the 1970s drew again on
these same principles. This book traces the evolution of this unwritten
law and shows its centrality to modern reorganization practice.

The first chapter of this book examines these principles in embryonic form by exploring how they operated in the wake of the financial
failure of Robert Morris at the end of the eighteenth century. Robert
Morris had been one of the richest and most prominent men in the
country, but he failed spectacularly and pulled many other once successful merchants down with him. This financial catastrophe drew
parties to the courthouse, where the judges had to begin with first
principles.

The second chapter connects these first principles to those that
judges adopted during the reorganization of the Atchison, Topeka,
and Santa Fe and the other great railroads that failed in the second
half of the nineteenth century. The benchmarks judges put in place
during this era established the ground rules for bargaining among
investors for the next several decades. Judges did not try to shape the
outcome of the negotiations. Instead, they ensured only that deals were

---

[6] An appellate case of recent vintage suggests that parties can make such payoffs, but its
reasoning is not compelling and its logic somewhat dubious. See In re Peabody Energy
Corp., 933 F.3d 918 (8th Cir. 2019).

struck honestly and in good faith. There had to be a process that gave everyone a fair opportunity to participate.

The third chapter turns from railroads and their investors to retail merchants and their suppliers at the start of the twentieth century. Railroads allowed long-distance trade to flourish. Not all small retailers were successful, however, and when they encountered trouble, it fell to the credit professionals who worked for their faraway and unpaid suppliers to sort things out. These credit men, as they called themselves, did not tolerate debtors whom they deemed unworthy, but they believed that it was appropriate to give some debtors a second chance. Their solicitude for these "worthy debtors" combined notions of honor and decency with self-interest.

The credit men had no patience for creditors who tolerated bad behavior, but neither did they think much of those who refused to make reasonable accommodations with worthy debtors. They pressed for legal reforms to provide a check against the forces that interfered with their efforts to reach a "friendly adjustment" of debt. In the process, they changed what behavior between debtor and creditor was acceptable and what was not.

In the 1930s, a group of New Deal reformers joined the investment bankers and the credit men to refashion the bargaining environment once again. The consensus that emerged during this decade is the focus of the book's fourth chapter. The New Deal reformers brought their own distinctive understanding of how judges were to oversee negotiations among creditors and their common debtor. Like their predecessors these reformers also invoked the Statute of 13 Elizabeth, but they interpreted its mandate more broadly. They believed that judges had to take steps to ensure that, at every turn, the bargaining process did not slight the rights of passive investors who had neither the information nor the sophistication to bargain on equal terms with Wall Street insiders.

The New Deal reformers were content to let the norms of credit men govern the rearrangement of the debt of small businesses, but they believed publicly traded firms were a different matter. They rejected the earlier wisdom that it was enough to ensure everyone had a seat at the bargaining table. For large firms, everyone's cards had to be face up on the table. Everyone had to put ulterior motives to one side and focus narrowly on their stake in the firm. Everything had to be done strictly according to Hoyle.

With the emergence of modern reorganization law in the 1930s, the absolute priority rule came into being. In contrast to what proceeded it, this priority regime cashed out the value of everyone's stake in the firm at the time of the reorganization. The fifth chapter shows that this idea emerged in large reorganizations not because of any belief in the intrinsic merit of recognizing absolute priority but only because New Deal reformers thought that such a priority rule best protected passive and unsophisticated investors from insiders. Giving each individual creditor the right to insist on being paid in full before anyone junior received anything, however, proved to be incompatible with achieving the mutually beneficial bargains that justified reorganization law in the first instance.

The sixth chapter looks at reorganization practice after the Second World War. The heavy regulatory oversight that New Deal reforms imposed on large firms was unsuccessful. Government regulators showed themselves insufficiently nimble. And the law depended too much on judicial valuations that proved too malleable and too uncertain. Moreover, although the credit men's commitment to accommodating worthy debtors worked tolerably well for small businesses, their norms offered judges no easy way to find their bearings elsewhere. Nowhere was this more evident than in real estate insolvencies.

The seventh chapter shows how the law changed dramatically during the 1970s. A group of skilled lawyers and academics returned to first principles and boldly reworked reorganization law once again. In their hands, the unwritten law that governs today took its modern form. These reformers focused squarely on creating an environment that was conducive to bargaining. Judges were to provide oversight, but they were no longer to do the heavy-handed policing upon which New Deal reformers had insisted. At the same time, however, judges had to embrace the basic norms of the credit men and do more than simply ensure that everyone had a seat at the table. Bargaining had to be forthright, and parties could not conceal conflicts of interest or advance private agendas.

The final chapter examines the challenges that have appeared over the last decade. New players and new capital structures make negotiations harder to manage. Applying old norms to novel practices is never easy. That said, today's bankruptcy judge continues to call upon the same core ideas that have been with us from the start. Side deals that corrupt or even cloud the process are forbidden. The judge is not a dispenser of Solomonic wisdom, but a referee who ensures a level playing field. The judge insists that the parties follow the rules, but does not enforce rules for their own sake, nor does the judge allow the oversight to interfere with the flow of play. In the end, judges leave it to the parties to find a path forward. If the parties cannot find a future for the firm, the judges will not do it for them.

This book differs from earlier accounts the law of corporate reorganization. Its focus is squarely on how the bankruptcy judge uses a set of unwritten rules, derived from fraudulent conveyance principles, to oversee the reorganization process.[7] By showing the central importance of these rules in modern reorganization practice and tracing how they have developed over time, this book provides entrée into a part of reorganization law that has been largely inaccessible.

This book also offers a more general lesson. The modern world is too complicated and changes too fast to expect ready answers from statutory text or established precedent. Judging is not simply a matter of calling balls and strikes. In every arena, judges must make sense of the various bits and pieces of the law. They need to find organizing principles that allow them to see a coherent picture. Many other areas of the law work or fail to work depending upon whether such principles

---

[7] There are, of course, a number of fine histories of bankruptcy law. One of the classics is Charles Warren, Bankruptcy in United States History (Harvard University Press 1935). In our own time, the gold standard remains David A. Skeel, Jr., Debt's Dominion: A History of Bankruptcy Law in America (Princeton University Press 2001). It should also be noted that the role that fraudulent conveyance doctrine has played in reorganization law has not been altogether ignored. See, e.g., Jerome N. Frank, Some Realistic Reflections on Some Aspects of Corporate Reorganization, 19 Va. L. Rev. 541, 542–46 (1933); Bruce A. Markell, Owners, Auctions, and Absolute Priority in Bankruptcy Reorganizations, 44 Stan. L. Rev. 69, 74–77 (1991).

This book focuses on how bankruptcy judges are empowered to police negotiations among the players. There is a separate debate about the extent to which bankruptcy judges are empowered to find substantive rights in the interstices of the Bankruptcy Code through their powers of common law adjudication. See, e.g., Adam Levitin, Toward a Federal Common Law of Bankruptcy: Judicial Lawmaking in a Statutory Regime, 80 Am. Bankr. L.J. 1 (2006); Jonathan M. Seymour, Against Bankruptcy Exceptionalism, 89 U. Chi. L. Rev. — (2022).

can be found and employed. Showing how one particular set of principles evolved and works in the case of corporate reorganizations makes it easier to identify and understand whether and how analogous forces are at work elsewhere.

Tracing the evolution of any set of ideas requires a return to the beginning. It is for that reason that this book starts on a dusty street in Philadelphia in 1801.

1 BADGES OF FRAUD

It is early evening in late August. The day began with fog, but the sky was clear by midmorning and the temperature rose steadily.[1] The heat of the day still lingers, but bright sunlight has turned a soft yellow-orange with the approach of twilight. Before us, emerging through a gateway, is a dignified, stout man in his late sixties. Robert Morris appears world-weary. He pauses to take stock of what lies behind and before him.

All the major events of his life have taken place within a short distance of where he stands. A block to the north is the State House, where Morris signed the Declaration of Independence, the Articles of Confederation, and the United States Constitution. Several blocks to the east on the riverfront lies the office Morris occupied when, as superintendent of finance, he served as the nation's first chief executive officer. The other department heads (and George Washington as commander in chief) reported to him there every Monday. But on this summer evening, the most immediate reminder to Morris of his past is the Prune Street Jail, which stands directly behind him. He has just spent three and a half years there, sorting through the debris of his many failed business deals.[2]

Morris's release from debtor's prison was not his own doing.[3] One of his creditors, a former business partner named John Huston, put him

---

[1] Charles Pierce, *A Meteorological Account of the Weather in Philadelphia from January 1, 1790 to January 1, 1847*, 151 (Lindsay & Blakiston 1847).
[2] For the details of Morris's time in the Prune Street Jail, see Charles Rappleye, *Robert Morris: Financier of the American Revolution*, 509–12 (Simon & Schuster 2010).
[3] See In re Morris, 17 F. Cas. 785, 791 (E.D. Pa. 1837); Bruce H. Mann, *Republic of Debtors: Bankruptcy in the Age of American Independence* 253 (Harvard University Press 2002).

into bankruptcy, and during this era an involuntary bankruptcy released debtors from prison, at least for a time. In theory, the bankruptcy might even end with a discharge of Morris's debts. But it likely will not. A discharge requires the blessing of his creditors, and there is little to suggest they are inclined to be magnanimous. Morris's defaults pulled a number of his creditors into debtor's prison with him and led to the financial ruin of quite a few others.

Morris's economic ruin and the simultaneous collapse of his one-time business partner provide a window into the world of debtors and creditors at the end of the eighteenth century. Morris's largest deal, a sale of a several thousand square mile parcel of land, is particularly instructive. The sale generated disputes among Morris, his many creditors, and the purchasers of the land. They involved the most prominent lawyers of the day, and the challenge of sorting out the ensuing complications implicated the core principles that still govern the relationship between distressed debtors and their creditors.

First, however, some background is necessary. Robert Morris dominated the economy of the early republic in a way that is almost impossible for us to fathom. Some sense of Morris's importance can be gleaned today by studying the frieze on the rotunda of the Capitol. It depicts the apotheosis of George Washington. Washington is surrounded by many Greek gods and a handful of mortals. One of them is Robert Morris.[4] His presence is no accident. Without Morris's help, the American Revolution would have failed. This was at least Washington's view.

Morris was the financier of the American Revolution. If he had not raised the money to pay reenlistment bonuses after the Battle of Trenton, Washington would not have been able to keep his army together.[5] Later in the war, when Morris was serving as superintendent of finance, Congress's credit was held in such low regard that Morris had to issue paper notes on which he as well as the United States was

---

[4] Morris's legacy can be found throughout the country in many other unexpected places. Visitors to Chicago's river walk will find Lorenzo Taft's statue of Morris and Washington at Heald Square. They are joined by Haym Salomon, another financier of the revolution. See https://en.wikipedia.org/wiki/Heald_Square_Monument.

[5] Rick Atkinson, *The British Are Coming: The War for America, Lexington to Princeton, 1775–1777* (Henry Holt & Co. 2019).

bound. His credit was better than the country's. These notes (nick-named "short Bobs" and "long Bobs")[6] were used to pay the Continental Army during the Battle of Yorktown.

At this time, Morris was one of the wealthiest men in the country. He had become rich trading and shipping goods. He exported wheat and other agricultural products of Pennsylvania, and he imported manufactured goods, wine, indentured servants, and occasionally slaves.[7] He had a network of agents on both sides of the Atlantic and established himself as an important trading partner. He used this network both to acquire supplies and munitions for the Continental Army and to engage in lucrative trade on his own behalf. In addition, Morris received letters of marque from the Continental Congress. These authorized him to put a fleet of privateers out to sea and seize British vessels.

For Morris, the relationship between entrepreneurship and patriot-ism was tight. When the *Commerce*, a particularly valuable merchant ship, was captured in June 1780, Morris and Blair McClenachan, a fellow merchant-privateer whose fortunes would remain linked to Morris, sent part of its cargo – a barrel of "what [was] deemed fine Spirits by good judges" – to George Washington as "a small token of the high esteem" in which they held him.[8] Washington responded with a characteristically gracious note a few weeks later, thanking them both for the liquor and their good wishes: "In a struggle like ours – perplexed with embarrassments – if it should be my fortune to conduct the Military helm in such a manner as to merit the approbation of good men and my suffering fellow Citizens, it will be the primary happiness of my life."[9]

In all his ventures, Morris took risks. In addition to securing deals throughout Europe and the Caribbean, he opened this country to trade with China and other countries in the Far East, partnering again with

---

[6] See Rappleye, supra note 2, at 258–59; Elizabeth M. Nuxoll, A Generation of Numismatic Co-Operation: Findings on the Notes and Coins of the Confederation Through the Papers of Robert Morris, 9 *American Journal of Numismatics*, 55, 81 (1997).

[7] Rappleye, supra note 2, at 24.

[8] Letter from Blair McClenachan and Robert Morris to George Washington, June 3, 1780.

[9] Letter from George Washington to Robert Morris and Blair McClenachan, June 20, 1780, from Springfield, NJ, available at https://issuu.com/nealauction/docs/nealauctioncatalog nov2010/33.

fellow merchants. Typical was a voyage of the ship *Canton* to India and back. For this venture, Morris partnered with John Huston, the man who later put him into bankruptcy (and who was also Blair McClenachan's son-in-law). The *Canton* left Philadelphia in the fall of 1789 with a cargo of bar iron, tar, pine lumber, porter, shrub, and Windsor chairs and returned sixteen months later with a cargo of spices and piece goods.[10]

Because of the risks he took, Morris's fortunes were always in flux. As with most traders, Morris's obligations outstanding at any moment in time vastly exceeded the value of the hard assets he had at his disposal. Keeping all the balls in the air required both skill and luck, and Morris's luck eventually ran out.

Morris's fortunes started to unravel during the Constitutional Convention in 1787.[11] Morris had bought enormous quantities of tobacco and had given bills of exchange to plantation owners in return. Bills of exchange were negotiable instruments that took the same form as a modern check, except that they were payable only many months after initial presentment and the party being ordered to pay was not a bank, but some other third party. In this case, it was Morris's agent in London. The sellers of tobacco were willing to accept Morris's bills in exchange for their tobacco because London merchants would in turn accept the bills as payment for goods that the plantation owners wanted.

Morris planned to sell the tobacco in France. The hard currency he would receive for the tobacco would enable his agent in London to honor the bills of exchange when they came due and still leave Morris with a substantial profit. At the start, nothing seemed amiss. Morris found buyers in France and entered into favorable contracts with them. It seemed that as long as they paid as promised, all would be well.

Things went wrong, however, when the first of these bills of exchange were presented to Morris's London agent. The London merchants had the right to ask the agent to "accept" the bills even though they were not yet due, and Morris's agent got cold feet. By accepting the bills, the agent would become personally liable on them,

---

[10] Eugene S. Ferguson, *Truxtun of the Constellation* 86–91 (Johns Hopkins Press 1956).
[11] See Rappleye, supra note 2, at 436.

and he was afraid that the French buyers would not pay Morris as they had promised, and he would have to honor the bills out of his own pocket when they became due. The agent refused to accept the bills, and this refusal was a default that accelerated Morris's obligation. Morris now had to pay the London merchants immediately, well before the French buyers were required to pay him. Morris had to scramble to find cash. The default damaged his reputation and made it harder for him to trade going forward.

Morris was never able to put out the fire that this default ignited. He engaged in ever-larger transactions. During the 1790s, Morris shifted his focus from importing and exporting goods to buying and selling real estate. At one time, he owned 40 percent of the building lots in the District of Columbia. His deals involving vast tracts on the frontier were even larger. Morris paid for the many parcels of land he acquired with negotiable instruments that he would be able to honor only if he could resell the land that he had bought for much more than he had paid.

Morris was able to turn over his initial land purchases at a substantial profit, and for a number of years he managed to honor his various obligations as they became due. But later transactions proved less successful. And then one of his partners cheated him. By the time he failed, Morris had issued more than $12 million in negotiable instruments. Morris's financial collapse coincided with renewed hostilities between the French and the British and an unwillingness of Europeans to invest in the United States.

Morris's failure pulled down many others with him. Those who received notes from Morris in return for their own goods used these notes to pay their own debts. They became liable on these debts again when Morris's notes were dishonored. There was financial misery for all those who had dealings with Morris or negotiated any of his notes. Morris bore considerable responsibility for putting the country into its worst financial crisis in its short history.

Morris's many creditors pursued him and eventually put him into debtor's prison. Putting a debtor in prison sometimes worked. The debtor or his friends might be able to pull together enough money to make peace with the creditors. But putting Morris in prison did little good. Morris's palatial houses (including one that George Washington used while president) were gone by this time, as were their lavish furnishings. Any hard assets creditors could seize were already in their hands. Morris's remaining assets were intangible. They consisted in large part of money others owed him, and many of Morris's own debtors were in debtor's prison with him.

Pennsylvania law gave Morris the ability to leave prison if he turned over all of his assets and made a complete accounting of his affairs, but Morris resolved on a different course. Even after he entered debtor's prison, Morris still hoped to untangle his financial affairs and put everything back in order. There was even a silver lining to being in debtor's prison. As long as Morris remained imprisoned, his creditors could not serve him with process, and he could continue to juggle his finances. Morris spent much of his time in prison sorting through his business affairs and finding various ways to support his family as well as himself.

Life in debtor's prison was neither solitary nor entirely uncomfortable. Morris had his own room with a window. It was large enough for a bed, table, couch, several desks, and eight chairs. Morris's wife and daughter could have dinner with him there, as could his old friends, including, on one occasion, George Washington.[12]

The transaction that Morris spent the most time unscrambling involved the sale of several thousand square miles of land in western New York (a tract that included all of what is now the city of Buffalo).[13] In the early 1790s, Morris had bought this land from the state of Massachusetts, subject to the claims of various Native American tribes.[14] He in turn sold most of the land to a consortium of Dutch investors still subject to the rights of the Native Americans. The Dutch investors had the option to treat the transaction either as a sale of the

---

[12] For a description of the dinner, see Ryan K. Smith, *Robert Morris's Folly: The Architectural and Financial Failures of an American Founder* 198 (Yale University Press 2014).

[13] In addition to sorting out the problems associated with the transaction, Morris had to placate the lawyer who represented the buyers of the land, as he owed him money as well. See Introductory Note: To Robert Morris, [18 March 1795], Founders Online, National Archives, https://founders.archives.gov/documents/Hamilton/01-18-02-0193-0001. See *The Papers of Alexander Hamilton, January 1795–July 1795*, vol. 18, 295–300 (Harold C. Syrett ed.) (Columbia University Press 1973).

[14] Charles E. Brooks, *Frontier Settlement and Market Revolution: The Holland Land Purchase* 13–14 (Cornell University Press 1996).

land to them or as a loan to Morris that was secured by a mortgage on the land.

By the time Morris entered debtor's prison, part of the picture had cleared. The complications that arose from the Native Americans' preemptive rights to the lands had been settled with the Treaty of the Big Tree,[15] and the Dutch investors had elected not to treat the transaction as a loan secured by a mortgage. Hence, all that was left was for Morris to execute a confirmation deed formally recognizing the transfer of ownership to the Dutch investors and erasing whatever errors might have been in the original deed.

On its face, it appeared that Morris no longer had any rights to the land, but Morris looked for a way to extract additional money from the Dutch investors.[16] An idea came to him from his son-in-law. He was a lawyer named James Marshall. Marshall would become a judge a few years later, and his brother would serve for many years as Chief Justice of the United States.[17] Marshall pointed out that the ability of the Dutch investors to treat the transaction as a loan backed up by a mortgage on the land might work in both directions. If the Dutch investors had the right to treat the deal as a loan, then Morris might have the option to treat it as a loan as well. In this event, Morris could return the purchase price to the Dutch investors and keep the land. To the extent that the value of the land exceeded this amount, he could enjoy the difference.

The land was likely not worth more than what the Dutch investors had paid for it, and Morris, of course, did not have access to the cash he would need to pay back the Dutch investors. Nevertheless, Morris, by asserting that he did have such a right, could put a cloud on the title. This might enable him to extract additional value from the Dutch investors. Before Morris could try to take advantage of the investors in this fashion, however, two groups of his creditors tried to stand in his place and shake down the Dutch investors themselves. They put

---

[15] See Smith, supra note 12, at 161.
[16] For an account of Morris's machinations here, see Paul Demund Evans, *The Holland Land Company* 177–85 (Buffalo Historical Society 1924).
[17] James Marshall is best remembered for being tasked with delivering a judicial commission to one William Marbury but failing to do so. This gave rise to his brother's most important opinion. See Marbury v. Madison, 5 U.S. 137 (1803).

separate liens on the New York property, and by doing this they hoped to use whatever leverage Morris had against the Dutch investors to their own advantage.

Particularly troublesome was the second group of creditors. They had bought claims against Morris at huge discounts after he had begun to default on his notes. Like distressed debt investors today, they did not expect payment in full. Instead, they hoped that, by placing liens on the New York property, they would be able to extract some money from both Morris and the Dutch investors. Among these speculators (and representing them in the negotiations with the Dutch investors and Morris) was a New York lawyer named Aaron Burr.

While in prison, Morris devised a way both to defeat Burr and to extract additional money from the Dutch investors. He began by asking a friend, Gouverneur Morris, to act on his behalf. No relation, Gouverneur Morris was a lawyer who had worked with Robert Morris while he was superintendent of finance and, like Morris, he was also a signatory to the United States Constitution. Indeed, he had written its preamble.

What followed was a series of negotiations and legal actions involving Morris, his lawyer, the various creditors who acquired the liens, and the Dutch investors. Of interest to us are the legal constraints that governed these negotiations. They capture in embryonic form the principles that remain at the core of the modern law of corporate reorganizations.

Gouverneur Morris persuaded the first (and more tractable) group of creditors to assign to him its claims against Robert Morris as well as its lien against the New York land in exchange for a token amount of money. Because this group was the first to acquire the lien, its rights to the land (that is, this group's rights to whatever rights Robert Morris still had in the land) were superior to Burr's. Hence, when Gouverneur Morris stepped into this group's shoes and proceeded to foreclose on the land, he acquired whatever rights Robert Morris still had in the land and, in the process, extinguished whatever rights Burr and his group had.

Gouverneur Morris then cut a deal with three lawyers in New York who were acting on behalf of the Dutch investors. (These were Alexander Hamilton and his partners, David A. Ogden and

Brockholst Livingston. Livingston would later serve on the Supreme Court of the United States.) Gouverneur Morris agreed to transfer to the Dutch investors the rights acquired at the foreclosure sale, and he also promised to have Robert Morris execute a confirmation deed that would reaffirm the rights conveyed in the original one. This would remove any and all doubts associated with the option or anything else related to the land. The Dutch investors in return paid Gouverneur Morris's expenses and promised to set up an annuity of $1,500 a year for Robert Morris's wife.

In short, through this series of transactions, the Dutch investors would have clean title to the land, Robert Morris's household would have additional income, and Aaron Burr and his confederates would be left with nothing. The pattern we observe here is one that we shall encounter many times. There is a conflict over an asset, or a group of assets owned or controlled by a hopelessly insolvent debtor. Negotiations among sophisticated parties follow, and they are greased by the promise of a side payment (in this case an annuity to Morris's wife). A deal is struck and those who were not party to the agreement are frozen out. The recurring question is whether such behavior violates the unwritten rules that govern such bargaining.

The world of Robert Morris was not populated by the weak or the unsophisticated. The principals were at home with transactions where the stakes were large. They were often speculators who acquired their positions at deep discounts. All were adults who affirmatively chose to play in the space and, as the presence of Aaron Burr illustrates, not always the most savory of human beings. The law was needed not to protect the weak, but rather to establish the terms of engagement.

In the accounting the bankruptcy forced Morris to provide his creditors, Morris attempted to put an innocent face on this transaction.[18] According to Morris, he had raised the issue of his right to repurchase the land, not to enrich himself, but only out of a sense of duty to his creditors. The entire issue was moot, Morris further argued, as the Dutch investors later acquired the judgment and execution originally levied against the land.[19] This statement was true

[18] Robert Morris, *Account of Robert Morris's Property* (King & Baird Printers 1801).
[19] Id., at 5–6.

as far as it went, but Morris neglected to note that it was one of his friends, acting as his agent, who had acquired rights to the land at the foreclosure sale and that it was this agent who had then sold these rights to the Dutch investors. He also made no mention of how, in the process, he had tried to divert additional value to himself via his wife.

Did Morris violate any laws in orchestrating this transaction? The threshold legal question was whether, in accounting for the transfer of the land, Morris had been sufficiently forthright. He had "to fully and truly disclose and discover all his ... effects and estate, real and personal" unless such property had been "really and bona fide before sold and disposed of, in the way of his trade ... and dealings."[20] If Morris in providing his account had failed to meet this mandate, he would be judged a "fraudulent bankrupt" and would lose the benefits of the act, including the hope of ever obtaining a discharge.

Courts in Philadelphia had wrestled with what constituted fraudulent behavior just a few years before. The question arose in the way of the failure of Morris's onetime business partner Blair McClenachan. McClenachan was the same person with whom, in happier times, Morris had commandeered British merchant vessels and shared the spoils with George Washington.

McClenachan's fortunes, like those of other Philadelphia merchants, took a turn for the worse in the 1790s in no small part thanks to Morris.[21] McClenachan gambled that Morris would successfully right his affairs. He made this bet (and doubled down on it) by acquiring several hundred thousand dollars of notes on which Morris was personally liable. He bought the notes first at 50 cents on the dollar, then at 30 cents, and then at 10 cents. Sometime afterward, McClenachan gave the notes to his children and their spouses. Just as some of his creditors were about to seize whatever they could find, McClenachan had his children return these notes to him in return for much of his real property.

After his term in Congress expired in 1799, McClenachan found himself with Morris in the Prune Street Jail. Unlike Morris, however, McClenachan tried to take advantage of Pennsylvania's insolvency

---

[20] §18, 1800 Bankruptcy Act.
[21] The background is set out in Ex parte Blair McClenachan, 2 Yeates 502 (Pa. 1799).

act.[22] This statute allowed McClenachan to leave prison if he gave up his property. And McClenachan was perfectly willing to turn over his assets, as they now consisted largely of the worthless notes of Morris he had reacquired from his children in return for his land.

The problem for McClenachan, however, was that relief under the statute was available only if he had not engaged in any actions that were a "fraud" against his creditors. McClenachan's trade of valuable land for notes of dubious value would not give rise to an ordinary action for fraud at common law, but the court found this was not dispositive. The court reached this conclusion by drawing on a principle that had emerged out of a statute Parliament passed in 1571, the thirteenth reginal year of Queen Elizabeth.[23]

That statute forbade transactions that "hinder, delay, or defraud" creditors. On its face, the law was aimed only at sham transactions that constituted ordinary fraud. A debtor attempted to thwart creditors by merely pretending to transfer assets to friends or relatives before absconding. Once creditors lost interest, the debtor planned to return and enjoy the assets once again. The statute gave courts the power to void such phantom transfers. Creditors could seize the assets from the friend or relative just as if they were still in the hands of the debtor. Each such transfer was a "fraudulent conveyance."

The sorts of transfers that were fraudulent conveyances, however, soon expanded beyond prohibiting out-and-out fraud. The turning point came in *Twyne's Case* in 1602. It held that, in addition to transactions involving actual fraud, the Statute of 13 Elizabeth empowered the court to strike down any transactions that had "badges of fraud."[24] Proof of outright fraud was not necessary. All that was required were indicia that a transaction was not an arm's-length deal in the marketplace. Badges of fraud could take many forms. One was the absence of

---

[22] The Statutes at Large of Pennsylvania from 1682 to 1801, vol. 16, p. 98, "An act providing that the person of a debtor shall not be liable to imprisonment for debt, after delivering up his estate for the benefit of his creditors, unless he hath been guilty of fraud or embezzlement."

[23] See 13 Eliz., ch. 5 (1571). The most enduring statute Parliament passed that year, it is commonly known simply as the Statute of 13 Elizabeth.

[24] For a comprehensive review of the case and the players involved, see Emily Kadens, New Light on *Twyne's Case*, 94 *Am. Bankr. L.J.* 1 (2020). It is also analyzed in Garrard Glenn, *Fraudulent Conveyances and Preferences* §§61–61e (Baker, Voorhis & Co. rev. ed. 1940).

12

reasonably equivalent value. A badge of fraud existed when a transaction was done secretly or when there was no physical transfer of assets or when the transaction did not serve any economic purpose.[25] The Statute of 13 Elizabeth became a place marker for the ability of a court to review suspicious transactions that undermined the rights of creditors. A court could declare them void and unwind them where appropriate.

The court followed these principles when it asked whether McClenachan's machinations with his children constituted "fraud" within the meaning of Pennsylvania's insolvency statute. The principles embedded in the Statute of 13 Elizabeth gave license to review all of a distressed debtor's transactions. Dealings intended to thwart creditors constituted "fraud" even if the elements of common law fraud were missing. The court held that McClenachan had forfeited his ability to invoke Pennsylvania's insolvency statute. Consistent with English precedents under the Statute of 13 Elizabeth, there was no need to make an inquiry into whether any actual fraud had been committed. As one of the justices put it, citing *King Lear*, "[N]o father, in full possession of reason, will put his estate in the power of his children, and render himself dependent on them, without sinister motives."[26]

It is possible that Robert Morris's machinations with the Dutch investors were "fraudulent" in the same way. Both Morris and McClenachan gave up value, and their relatives benefited at the expense of their creditors. McClenachan's children end up with land, Morris's wife the promise of an annuity. But there was a critical difference. McClenachan owned the land that he transferred to his children. Morris, however, never had the annuity. He never gave or promised anything to his wife. The Dutch investors did.

A court would have had little trouble if Robert Morris had extracted money from the Dutch investors and then gave that money to his wife. Such a gift would have stood on the same footing as McClenachan's purported transfer of real property to his children. It would in all events

---

[25] As Justice Cardozo explained in Shapiro v. Wilgus, 287 U.S. 348, 354 (1932), "A conveyance is illegal if made with an intent to defraud the creditors of the grantor, but equally it is illegal if made with an intent to hinder and delay them."

[26] Ex parte Blair McClenachan, 2 Yeates 502, 507 (Pa. 1799).

have to be disclosed. But value never passed from the Dutch investors into Morris's hands. The question then concerns the sort of scrutiny that a court should give to the transaction as a whole: a transaction that involved a number of steps, including a foreclosure sale, followed by a promise of a transfer from the Dutch investors to the wife that bypassed Morris altogether.

The Dutch investors acted in good faith, and this might seem to distinguish Morris's dealings with them from McClenachan's dealings with his children. As far as the dealings between Morris and the Dutch investors were concerned, everything was done at arm's length. But the presence of good faith on the part of those who received property from the debtor was not enough to insulate a transaction from the reach of the principle at the heart of the Statute of 13 Elizabeth.

Another transaction involving McClenachan shows that this much was already clear at the start of the nineteenth century. At about the same time that McClenachan conveyed much of his land to his children in exchange for notes signed by Robert Morris, McClenachan also transferred his other land to several men to hold in trust for the benefit of his creditors.[27] On the face of it, McClenachan, far from evading creditors, was putting in place a mechanism to pay them. The court in this case, *Burd v. Smith*, explicitly found that the facts "acquit[ted] Mr. McClenachan of any intentional, or mental, fraud."[28]

Nevertheless, the justices who reviewed this transaction found that it too was inconsistent with the principles embodied in the Statute of 13 Elizabeth notwithstanding the absence of actual fraud. The court grounded its conclusion on an opinion from England decided just a few decades before. That case involved a person who loaned a friend a large amount of money in order to help him sort out his business affairs. A few days after he received the loan, the friend realized that he could no longer save his business. He returned the money and then fled to France. The creditors started a bankruptcy proceeding and sought to recover the repayment. The loan had been made in good faith, and the lender's behavior was impeccable. But

---

[27] Burd v. Smith, 4 U.S. 76 (Pa. 1802).
[28] 4 U.S. at 86.

Lord Mansfield, among the most eminent judges in the common law tradition, held that this payment was void nevertheless.

At the outset, Lord Mansfield conceded that ordinarily a debtor can prefer one creditor over another.[29] Moreover, he recognized that, even when a debtor's back is against the wall, the debtor can make transfers to creditors who demand payment or sue or otherwise press for repayment. But Mansfield found that debtors themselves are no longer free to favor one creditor or another as they are absconding.

Lord Mansfield acknowledged that the creditor was "very meritorious." But this was of no moment. A debtor is no longer free to make transfers after engaging in acts that undermine the rights of creditors. There is no actual fraud, but such preferential payments nevertheless "hinder, delay, or defraud" other creditors within the meaning of the Statute of 13 Elizabeth.

Harman v. Fishar provided the wellspring for the power the trustee enjoys today to recover payments made to creditors on the eve of bankruptcy.[30] In addition, the court in *Burd v. Smith* found in Lord Mansfield's opinion a much broader principle. A payment of a completely legitimate debt or some other arm's-length transaction could violate the rights of creditors, even if no bankruptcy was in the offing. Even though *Harman* involved a payment made in connection with a bankruptcy, the idea that a payment to a creditor could violate the Statute of 13 Elizabeth applied whenever a debtor was under pressure. Financially distressed debtors had to cut square corners.

There was no bankruptcy law in place in the United States at the time. (Congress did not pass a bankruptcy statute until 1800, three years after this transaction.[31]) The court conceded that a preference without more, even when a debtor is distressed, was unobjectionable:

> There can be no doubt . . . of the right of a debtor (and cases may be easily conceived, in which it would be a duty) . . . to give a preference to some of his creditors, in exclusion of the rest; and,

---

[29] Harman v. Fishar (1774) 98 Eng. Rep. 998, 1001; 1 Cowp. 118, 123.

[30] Bankruptcy Code §547. For the canonical analysis of the evolution of preference law, see Robert Weisberg, Commercial Morality, the Merchant Character, and the History of the Voidable Preference, 39 *Stan. L. Rev.* 3 (1986).

[31] Act of April 4, 1800, ch. 19, 2 Stat. 19 (repealed 1803).

from such a preference alone, the Court would not be disposed, hastily, to infer collusion, secret trusts, or meditated frauds.[32]

Nevertheless, the court found that McClenachan's transfer of land to a trust for the benefit of his creditors was ineffective. Various things McClenachan failed to do – such as call a meeting of his creditors or create a schedule of his assets or make some of the creditors' trustees or explain to them how he would go about distributing the assets – suggested that McClenachan set up the trust as a way to defeat the creditors who were about to secure judgments against him. There were enough badges of fraud to require voiding the transaction.

The justices in Pennsylvania identified in the Statute of 13 Elizabeth a general principle that extended beyond preferential transfers on the eve of bankruptcy. As long as a transaction was made with a view to hinder a creditor, it could be voided. McClenachan could not purport to create a vehicle for paying off some creditors if he did it in order to undermine the rights of other creditors. As one of the justices explained:

> I cannot conceive anything more dangerous, than to sanction by a judicial determination, a deed of this description. It will be vesting the debtor with unlimited power at all times over his property, to baffle his creditors, under the specious pretext of paying them.[33]

Burd v. Smith is one of the earliest instantiations of the idea that transactions rearranging the rights of a debtor and bona fide creditors are themselves subject to judicial scrutiny. This idea is not manifest on the face of the Statute of 13 Elizabeth and exists nowhere else in any statute, yet it is a principle firmly embedded in the law. A judge possesses inherent ability to assess the conduct of the debtor and strike down transactions that are designed to undermine the rights of one or more of the creditors. When a debtor assigns assets for the benefit of creditors, courts have the power, and indeed the duty, to police the transaction and make sure that all is as it should be.

The logic of this opinion casts a shadow over Morris's transaction with the Dutch investors. It suggests that Robert Morris was obliged to

---

[32] 4 U.S. at 86.
[33] 4 U.S. at 89.

disclose the various dealings between Gouverneur Morris and the Dutch investors on the ground that Gouverneur Morris was his agent, and the dealings were not "bona fide."[34]

Imagine a simpler version of the transaction: Robert Morris himself, rather than Gouverneur Morris, had purchased the New York land at the foreclosure sale. After acquiring again all the rights he had in the land before the two groups of creditors levied on it, Morris then conveyed these rights to the Dutch investors in return for their promise to give his wife $1,500 a year.[35] In such a case, creditors could invoke the same principles that Blair McClenachan's creditors invoked when he purported to transfer his assets to receivers. Morris was engaging in a transaction in order to put an asset (his remaining rights to several thousand square miles of land) beyond the reach of his creditors. If the Dutch investors had not yet given Morris's wife the annuity, they had to give it to the creditors instead.

Burd v. Smith captures the idea that, as long as creditors can identify a particular asset that the debtor tried to keep from them (land in the case of McClenachan or the rights acquired at the foreclosure in this simple version of Robert Morris's transaction), courts possess the power to unwind the transaction or recover its value. This idea took firm root during the course of the nineteenth century. The Supreme Court ultimately confronted just such a case in *Chicago, Rock Island & Pacific Railroad Co. v. Howard* in 1868.[36]

The Mississippi & Missouri Railroad was hopelessly insolvent. By all accounts, there was not enough value to pay its senior creditors in full. The senior creditors wanted to foreclose on the railroad's assets and sell them to a third party, but those in control of the railroad could put numerous obstacles in their way. The senior creditors wanted to clear a smooth path to a sale, just as the Dutch investors wanted clean title to the land in upstate New York. Those in control of the railroad promised to cooperate if, in return, the senior creditors allowed part of

---

[34] §10, 1800 Bankruptcy Act.
[35] See Evans, supra note 16, at 184. An extended discussion of the annuity, with references to contemporaneous correspondence, can be found in the notes to a letter from Gouverneur Morris to Alexander Hamilton, August 31, 1802, see https://founders.archives.gov/documents/Hamilton/01-26-02-0001-0037, shortly after Robert Morris left prison.
[36] 74 U.S. 392 (1868).

the proceeds to go to the old shareholders. Meanwhile, the general creditors of the old corporation would be left with nothing.

The senior creditors faced the same difficulties as the Dutch investors. The old shareholders of the railroad stood to those in control of a corporate debtor as Morris's wife stood to him. The senior creditors were dealing with people in a position to make trouble (those in control of the railroad), and peace came at a price. Instead of someone for whom the debtor has affection (Morris's wife) receiving an annuity, those whom those in control favored (the old shareholders) were to receive new securities.

The Supreme Court had little difficulty in *Howard* insisting that the general creditors of the Mississippi & Missouri were entitled to the proceeds that the buyer of the railroad had promised to the old shareholders. To be sure, the case would have been utterly different if the senior creditors had foreclosed without any help from the shareholders. The amount realized from the foreclosure sale would not have been enough to pay the senior creditors in full, and hence these senior creditors could have kept all of it. In the same way, the Dutch investors might have acquired all of the land if they had ignored Gouverneur Morris and instead established in court that Morris had no remaining rights in the land. But once they enlisted the help of the debtor in return for a share of the proceeds, matters are altogether different. The debtor (or wife or shareholders of the debtor) cannot pocket value while the creditors receive nothing.

Howard appears to rely on a now-discredited notion Justice Story developed in *Wood v. Dummer*.[37] In that case, Story suggested that the capital shareholders initially contribute to a corporation is held in trust for the benefit of the corporation's creditors. But the better understanding of Justice Story's opinion (and *Howard*) is found elsewhere. *Dummer* is not usually seen through the lens of the Statute of 13 Elizabeth, but it should be.[38] Even though the corporation in *Dummer* was solvent, it was nevertheless wrapping up its affairs. It requires no notions of trust law to find that distributions from

---

[37] See Wood v. Dummer, 30 F. Cas. 435, No. 17,944, 3 Mason 308 (1824) (Story, Circuit Justice).

[38] This account of *Howard* as resting on fraudulent conveyance principles is not new. See Frank, supra note 7, at 569.

a liquidating firm to its shareholders that put its ability to pay creditors at risk are problematic. Those running a firm and its shareholders are often one and the same. When those in control of a firm transfer its assets to shareholders they stand in the same position as when someone like Morris or McClenachan transfers assets to a relative. The liquidation of a corporation in a way that benefits shareholders at the expense of creditors should trigger scrutiny for the same reason. Leakage of value to shareholders when a corporation is wrapping up is a badge of fraud.

We have been considering a variation on the facts surrounding Morris's machinations with the Dutch investors that differs from the facts of the case in several ways that might seem to matter. For one thing, this variation assumes that Morris dealt directly with the Dutch investors, and in the actual case Morris acted through an intermediary. Robert Morris was not the one who acquired rights to the New York land at a foreclosure sale. Instead, it was Gouverneur Morris.

This wrinkle alone was sufficient to insulate the transaction from searching scrutiny in a later piece of related litigation that ultimately reached the Supreme Court.[39] That this litigation never brought Robert Morris's machinations to light is relatively easy to explain. Robert Morris was dead by then. Moreover, the principal creditor whom Morris had frozen out (Aaron Burr) was living in exile in England (in order to evade his own creditors). It was left to others to advance the case (yet another group of creditors Morris failed to pay). In addition, Burr had killed the principal lawyer representing the Dutch investors on the other side of the transaction (Alexander Hamilton). Moreover, only five of the seven justices sitting on the Supreme Court at the time heard this case. The chief justice was absent. (Recall that the Chief Justice's brother, James Marshall, was Morris's son-in-law and had helped Morris concoct the scheme in the first place.) Nor did Associate Justice Livingston hear the case. (Recall too that he had represented the Dutch investors with his now-late partner, Alexander Hamilton.)

But even if one treats Gouverneur Morris simply as an agent of Robert Morris, the transaction with the Dutch investors had an additional

---

[39] Fitzsimmons v. Ogden, 11 U.S. 2, 7 Cranch 2 (1812).

element that makes it different from transactions that are fraudulent conveyances within the net of the Statute of 13 Elizabeth. On its face, the Statute seems to require a transfer of property from the debtor. Morris himself promised the Dutch investors only a confirmation deed, a deed that would affirm the earlier conveyance of land and remove any cloud the transaction might be under given the option. The confirmation deed would do little more than ensure that Morris would make no trouble for the Dutch investors later on. A promise to execute such a deed might not rise to the level of a transfer of a property interest. Without a transfer of property, it might seem there could be no fraudulent conveyance.

We need to ask whether the creditors of Morris could reach the annuity even if Morris had never transferred a cognizable property interest to the Dutch investors. The Dutch investors bought his cooperation. His cooperation might not have been an asset transferred to them in the sense that cooperation on his part was not anything that his creditors could seize, convert to cash, and use to satisfy a debt.

The same problem would have arisen in *Howard* if the transaction had been structured differently. Assume that, instead of the buyer agreeing to pay part of the consideration for the railroad to the old senior creditors and the other part to the old shareholders, the buyer had promised to give the entire consideration to the senior creditors, and the senior creditors then made a separate promise to the shareholders.

The senior creditors were owed more than the value of the land, and they were entitled to the entire consideration received from the sale. They were at all times free to give their own property to whomever they pleased. In this event, there would be no property that came *from the debtor's hands* to the shareholders. There was nothing that belonged to the debtor that was going to the shareholders.

Under this variation on *Howard*, the general creditors would have to confront the same problem that Robert Morris's creditors would have had to face if they had sought to reach the annuity and Morris had merely promised his cooperation to the Dutch investors and had not given them a cognizable property interest. In this event, the shareholders are receiving value only from the senior creditors. The debtor corporation itself never gave anything to its shareholders.

Morris and the corporation had enough control over assets (rights to New York land on the one hand and the railroad on the other) to keep others entitled to those assets (the Dutch investors and the senior creditors respectively) from reaching them. Both Morris and the corporation used their ability to put obstacles in the way of rightful owners. Both the Dutch investors and the senior creditors were willing to pay to have these obstacles go away. And both Morris and the corporation reached a deal in which the respective third parties agreed to divert value not to them, but rather to others close to them (Morris's wife in the first case and the shareholders in the second).

The shareholders in this variation on *Howard* are receiving money from the senior creditors because those sympathetic to them (the managers of the corporation) are able to make life hard for the senior creditors, just as Morris's wife is receiving the annuity because Morris has the ability to make life hard for the Dutch investors. Under these facts, the shareholders, like Morris's wife, are profiting from the ability of someone in control to grease the skids.

This ability to grease the skids is not, strictly speaking, an asset of the debtor. The general creditors of a corporation have no way to force those who controlled it to shake down others, just as Morris's general creditors had no way to force Morris to shake down the Dutch investors. The money the Dutch investors gave Morris's wife was never Morris's "property." Similarly, the money that the shareholders receive from the senior creditors in this variation on the facts never belonged to the corporation.

The question becomes whether a transfer of property from the debtor is a necessary condition to invoking fraudulent conveyance principles. It was not raised either in *Howard* or in Morris's bankruptcy. The facts in *Howard* itself did involve a transfer of property to the debtor and then to a third party, so the question of whether such a transfer was essential was never before the court. Such a question would have been before the court in Morris's bankruptcy if properly raised, but it was not.

The person taking the lead in Morris's bankruptcy was John Huston. In addition to being Morris's business partner in the India venture, Huston was the son-in-law of Blair McClenachan. He was himself facing hard times. He still had or had reacquired the Morris notes that McClenachan had bought at a steep discount and subsequently gave Huston and his wife (McClenachan's daughter). Huston still hoped to get something for them. But neither he nor the many other creditors of Morris who were involved in his bankruptcy were up to the challenge that Morris presented them.

The account Morris provided his creditors ran for seventy-four printed pages, and Huston and the other creditors were not able to parse it. They did not see that the account Morris provided of the transaction with the Dutch investors was less than completely forthright. The web of transactions it set out was sufficiently intricate that Huston and the others either did not see through it or concluded that the cost of unraveling his deals exceeded anything they would receive at the end of the day.[40] They never learned about the Dutch investors' promise to give Morris's wife an annuity. They threw up their hands, abandoned the bankruptcy proceeding, and gave Morris a discharge. The bankruptcy case itself continued rudderless for many decades,[41] and whatever assets were to be had wasted away.

Robert Morris was able to live the rest of his life outside of prison, but the Dutch investors had the last laugh. Once they received the rights that Gouverneur Morris had acquired, they realized that they had no need for Robert Morris's continuing cooperation or the confirmation deed, and hence they never kept their promise to give his wife an annuity.

The principle that empowered courts to review dealings between debtors and their creditors remained in an embryonic state. The basic shape of the principle was already in place, however. Courts looked at transactions involving distressed debtors holistically. Courts could strike down a suspect transfer of land Blair McClenachan purportedly made for the benefit of his creditors without pointing to any actual fraud. But exactly when and under what circumstances courts could use their power to prevent transactions when there was mischief on the side was not yet clear. The issue did, however, come into full focus with the rise of equity receiverships at the end of the nineteenth century, and it is to this story that the next chapter turns.

---

[40] See Morris, supra note 18.
[41] See In re Morris, 17 F. Cas. 785 (E.D. Pa. 1837).

2 A SEAT AT THE TABLE

At the end of the nineteenth century, courts once again confronted the question of how to oversee distressed debtors as they try to sort out their affairs with their creditors. The reorganization of the great railroads of this era forced courts once again to draw on the Statute of 13 Elizabeth and the principles at work in McClenachan's insolvency and later in *Howard*. A new understanding emerged after considerable debate.

To appreciate the stakes, it is necessary to look at the challenges that investors in railroads faced at the end of the nineteenth century. These were quite different from those of the creditors who had dealings with the likes of Robert Morris. The reorganization of the Atchison, Topeka, and Santa Fe provides a useful point of entry.

In the early 1860s, Cyrus Holliday envisioned a railroad that would stretch across southern Kansas. The railroad would begin in Atchison on the Missouri River, proceed to Topeka, and continue southwest to the state border in the direction of Santa Fe.[1] Holliday had grand visions of a transcontinental railroad extending from the Missouri River to both the Pacific Ocean and the Gulf of Mexico, but for three decades the operations of the onomatopoeic Atchison, Topeka, and Santa Fe were squarely focused on Kansas.

To carry out his vision, Holliday obtained a land grant from Congress and raised money from individual counties and private investors. But he soon had to seek out investors on the East Coast,

---

[1] Keith L. Bryant, *History of the Atchison, Topeka and Santa Fe Railway* 10 (Macmillan Publishing Co. 1974).

primarily in Boston, and later abroad, primarily in England. These investors soon took control of the railroad and continued to expand it. Kidder Peabody, an investment bank founded in Boston in 1865, raised much of the capital. In the early 1870s, it sold each share of stock in the railroad for $100. To create a demand for the stock at that price, it had to offer bonds as a bonus. Those who invested $10,000 in the Atchison, Topeka, and Santa Fe would receive 100 shares of stock and a package of bonds with a face amount of a little more than $14,000 that paid about $1,000 each year.[2]

Over the next two decades, the Atchison, Topeka, and Santa Fe (AT&SF) expanded, building short lines off the main lines throughout Kansas and extending the main lines to the west, the south, and the east. In many cases, these lines were placed in subsidiary corporations. The subsidiaries issued their own bonds, and the AT&SF guaranteed them. The AT&SF sometimes acquired railroads already built by others and held them in subsidiaries as well.

Those who owned bonds of the AT&SF and its subsidiaries were not like holders of Robert Morris's notes. Until the end, Morris's notes were treated like money. Indeed, at times, they were more valuable than the notes of the United States. They represented a promise of payment that was to be honored on pain of going to prison if the promise were broken. They were typically used to buy goods from other merchants. Morris's notes created a vast interlocking web of debtors and creditors.

By contrast, those who gave money to the AT&SF were investors in a common venture. They understood from the start that they would get their money back only if the railroad generated revenue over and above its operating expenses. Each railroad bond was simply a deal between the railroad and its investors. The investors gave the railroad cash and the railroad in return gave them rights to the cashflows, if any, that the railroad generated.

There was at least one more difference worth stressing. Robert Morris's business did not have an identity apart from him. A large railroad was different. It existed apart from those who were running it at any moment in time. Once a firm reached a certain size, no single individual was essential. Moreover, professional managers often saw

[2] Id., at 23.

their loyalties running to the business itself rather than to its founder or any particular group of investors. Suppliers and customers similarly saw their relationship with the firm apart from their relationship with any individual who worked for it. Once a firm was the size of a nineteenth-century railroad, it had its own identity, apart from the people who ran it or owned it.

Cyrus Holliday continued to serve on the board of the AT&SF for many decades, but he stopped making operational decisions relatively early on. After the AT&SF overcame some growing pains in the early 1870s, it flourished for years under the leadership of professional managers who were not themselves investors in the railroad. They served at the pleasure of the board, and when the board decided that someone else could do their jobs better, they were replaced. Nevertheless, they controlled the day-to-day operations of the business, and they were the ones charged with presenting new initiatives.

A. A. Robinson came to the AT&SF in 1871 and quickly moved up the ranks.[3] William Barstow Strong worked for a number of railways before he came to the AT&SF in 1877 as general manager.[4] He became president in 1881 and worked hand-in-glove with Robinson. They modernized the AT&SF. They replaced iron rails with steel ones, built many new bridges, and acquired new equipment. By 1889, AT&SF had lines that extended from Chicago to San Diego on the Pacific and to Galveston on the Gulf of Mexico. And AT&SF had fourteen wholly owned subsidiaries. In addition to controlling twenty-five railroads and 6,443 miles of track, it exercised joint control over four other railroads and 517 miles of track. The AT&SF had grown large, too large.

Strong and Robinson had, in retrospect, overestimated the benefits of having an integrated system. The Atlantic & Pacific Railroad (A&P) connecting the system to the Pacific lost huge amounts of money, as did the railroad connecting the system to Chicago. It would be more profitable for AT&SF to lease track or use another railroad to connect to the West Coast than to run its own line. Similarly, it made more sense

---

[3] L. L. Waters, *Steel Trails to Santa Fe* 46 (University of Kansas Press 1950).
[4] Id., at 54.

to link up with any one of the four railroads that ran from Kansas to Chicago than to own and operate a railroad of its own.

At the same time, the AT&SF faced increased competition from other railroads, and bad farming conditions reduced the volume of agricultural products that it carried. In addition, state regulators in Kansas and the newly formed national regulatory agency, the Interstate Commerce Commission, came into being. They reduced the rates the railroad could charge.

By 1889, the AT&SF's net operating earnings each year were no longer sufficient to meet $11.2 million in fixed charges on forty-one different bond issues.[5] The investors, represented by Kidder Peabody, forced dramatic changes. Strong and Robinson were replaced with managers who, the investors believed, would be more fiscally prudent. To put the railroad's fiscal house in order, there was an exchange offer. Holders of most of its outstanding bonds were given the chance to trade their bonds for some combination of two new ones, the first paying 4 percent interest and the other 4 percent only when earned. The vast majority of the existing bondholders agreed to the exchange. As a result, the capital structure of the railroad was dramatically simplified, and its fixed charges fell to $7.4 million annually.[6] At this point, the railroad's capital structure (apart from guarantees to bondholders of its A&P subsidiary and some lease obligations) consisted of two classes of bonds and then common stock.

In the wake of these changes, the fortunes of the railroad improved so much that the new managers converted the junior bonds that paid out only if the railroad generated enough income to ones that paid a fixed rate of interest.[7] A number of new investors acquired the junior bonds. Investors in London owned nearly half of them by the end of 1893.[8]

At this point, however, the country experienced one of the worst economic recessions in its history. Traffic on the road fell again. The

---

[5] Eighteenth Annual Report of the Board of Directors to the Stockholders of the Atchison, Topeka & Santa Fe Railroad Company for the Fiscal Year Ended June 30, 1890, at pp. 23–25.

[6] Id., at 25.

[7] Stuart Daggett, *Railroad Reorganization* 206 (Harvard University Press 1908).

[8] Id., at 206.

AT&SF generated only $6 million a year in operating profits, and this was no longer enough to meet the $7.4 million due in interest payments each year. The railroad needed a new capital structure that would bind all creditors, and it was plain that the managers would no longer be able to approach the old investors and persuade them to trade in their old securities for new ones. Too many would resist the haircut needed to put the AT&SF on a sound footing. Given that something close to unanimity was not possible, the AT&SF needed a legal process that would allow it to create a new capital structure. Hence, it needed to put itself into an equity receivership.

The equity receivership was a peculiar legal procedure that had become the tool of choice for giving a railroad a new capital structure when the presence of too many recalcitrant investors prevented an exchange offer from working.[9] To begin an equity receivership, the railroad's lawyers would find a general creditor who was willing to help the railroad. That creditor would sue the railroad in a well-disposed federal court, declaring that it had not been paid and asking the judge to order all of the railroad's assets to be transferred to a receiver to be sold. The railroad would not contest the motion.

At this point, the creditor would ask for specific individuals (suggested to it by the railroad itself) to be appointed receivers. In the case of the AT&SF, the creditor suggested the appointment of the AT&SF's current CEO, the railroad's general counsel, and a respected businessman as receivers.

The receivers then conducted what was in form a sale of the assets. Of course, no single buyer could amass the millions of dollars that the AT&SF was still worth, but a committee that held the proxies of the senior bondholders would appear and "credit-bid." The committee would offer to buy the railroad and offer in exchange the debt it was owed.

The most senior creditors of the railroad were entitled to all the proceeds of the sale up to the amount of their claim. Even without credit bidding, a committee that held all the senior claims, in theory at least, could simply borrow an amount equal to its senior claims for

---

[9] For an excellent account of the workings of the equity receivership, see David A. Skeel, Jr., *Debt's Dominion: A History of Bankruptcy Law in America* 48–70 (Princeton University Press 2001).

a few minutes and use this cash to bid for the railroad. No one else would put in a competing bid, and the senior committee would win the auction. As the winner of the auction, the committee became the owner of the railroad. A few moments later, the receiver would also return the cash to the committee. As the holder of the senior claims, the committee was entitled to the proceeds of the auction. The committee could then use this cash to repay the loan. In principle, all these steps could be done in minutes or seconds. In the blink of an eye, the committee would have the railroad, and the money would be back in the hands of the lender.

Credit bidding merely relieved the senior committee from incurring the costs associated with obtaining this short-term loan. It did not change the outcome of the auction. Round-tripping of cash would serve no particular purpose beyond imposing a barrier to an effective reorganization, at least in the view of the professionals involved.

In practice, matters were only somewhat more complicated. The senior committee did not hold all the senior claims. There were usually holdouts, and the senior committee could credit bid only the portion of senior claims that they held. They had to put up cash for the rest. If the senior committee held 90 percent of the senior claims, they would need to put up 10 percent in cash. Because the senior committee was the only bidder, the price it bid was artificially low, and it was able to cash out senior creditors who did not turn their claims over to the committee at a fraction of their value.

Even though the holders of the senior bonds might be widely dispersed, organizing them usually proved relatively easy. Many of the investors acquired their bonds through investment banks such as Kidder Peabody, and these same investment bankers acted on their behalf during the reorganization. There were others, such as insurance companies (New York Life in the case of AT&SF), who held large positions and hired professionals to represent them. Once a critical mass turned over their proxies to the "protective committee" that represented the senior investors in the reorganization process, all who had not yet joined had a powerful incentive to do so, given that, if they did not join, they could be cashed out at a large discount. And it made even more sense for junior investors to join their protective committee.

An example will make it clear why it was in every investor's interest to join the protective committee formed to represent its class of bond once the senior protective committee acquired a substantial number of proxies. Assume the senior protective committee controlled 90 percent of the class. With this much control, it had to put up only 10 percent of its bid in cash. It could credit-bid the balance. And its bid could be quite low relative to the value of the railroad. In the absence of any competing bid, the senior committee would need only to exceed the artificially low "upset price" that the court established.

Even if the railroad was worth $125 million, the court might set the upset price at $10 million. As long as no other bidders appeared at the auction, the senior committee could acquire the railroad with a bid of $10 million and put up only $1 million in cash. The receiver would give the assets of the railroad to the senior committee (as the high bidder) and distribute the $1 million of the bid that was not a credit bid to the creditors who did not join the committee.

In short, the 10 percent of senior creditors who did not give the committee their proxies would receive only $1 million, even though the value of their stake in the firm was worth $12.5 million (10 percent of a railroad worth $125 million). Faced with the choice between joining the protective committee or receiving only a token cash payment for their senior claim, most chose to join. And, of course, holders of junior securities had an even greater incentive to join their committees. If they joined, the plan gave them something. If they did not, they would receive nothing.

After the "sale," the senior protective committee owned all the assets of the railroad, and it could do with them whatever it pleased. In the ordinary case, it would distribute new securities in the railroad according to a plan that it had reached with the various junior committees. Under the typical agreement, each investor would emerge with new securities that were roughly equal to the value of the investor's claim against the railroad in the absence of a reorganization. If there were equal amounts of senior and junior debt and senior debt was trading at 70 and junior debt was trading at 30, the seniors would receive securities equal to 70 percent of the value of the reorganized business and the juniors would receive 30 percent. The reorganization left them with different securities, but they were worth roughly the same amount, as would have been the case in the event of an exchange offer.

The principal qualification to preserving the value that all investors held in the railroad was that a norm emerged that junior security holders, typically the old equityholders, had to pay for the costs of the reorganization. These would include both the fees of the professionals and the money needed to pay the senior bondholders who did not give their proxies to the senior protective committee.

The central problem that emerged during the era of the equity receivership was exactly what oversight that court had to give to this process. The auction the receiver conducted, of course, was an auction in form only. It merely facilitated the recapitalization. Seen at a high level of generality, an equity receivership was a transaction orchestrated by the debtor in which assets were turned over to investment bankers and then distributed to the various creditors, junior and senior, on terms that the debtor and the investment bankers found agreeable. Put in this fashion, the debtor's participation raised concerns similar to the ones found in *Burd v. Smith*. In both cases, a distressed debtor found breathing space by purporting to transfer assets for the benefit of creditors, while still retaining control. Nor is a receivership so different from what went on in *Howard*. There was a sale and the old share-holders ended up with a stake in the firm while some of the creditors (in this case those who did not join one of the committees) were left out in the cold.

That each discrete transaction was regular in form (the receiver-ship; the foreclosure sale; the distribution of new securities by the high bidder at the sale) did not itself insulate the reorganization as a whole from scrutiny. Courts had to look to substance rather than form and decide whether the entire transaction passed muster or instead pos-sessed sufficient badges of fraud that it could be struck down as a fraudulent conveyance. If the reorganization process as a whole was tainted by suspect dealings, the court had to use its power to prevent it from going forward. It was the responsibility of the court to connect all the dots and ensure the integrity of the process as a whole. It did not limit its focus to specific transfers of property from the debtor.

None of this was in dispute. Everyone accepted that courts were there to ensure that debtors were transparent and forthright in their dealings with their creditors. What was contested, however, was how hard a look was required in the context of a corporate reorganization. Nothing after all was written down.

A key actor in the AT&SF receivership was Victor Morawetz, a thirty-four-year-old lawyer who had already established himself as one of the country's leading authorities on corporate law. Morawetz is not well known today, but in skill and intellect he was as able as any who came before or since. Born in Baltimore, he quickly made himself at home in the world. Morawetz received a rigorous education in Europe, mastered French, German, and Spanish, and became a first-class violinist. By the time he turned seventeen, he had already served as an aide-de-camp during the Third Carlist War in Spain and, while on duty there, had been a special war correspondent for the *Baltimore Gazette*.[10]

Morawetz returned to the United States, graduated from Harvard Law School at twenty-one, and then began a law practice in Chicago. During his time in Chicago, he wrote the first American treatise on corporate law. This brought him to the attention of Andrew Carnegie. Morawetz moved to New York, did legal work for Carnegie there, and then became an associate at the law firm of Seward, Da Costa, & Guthrie in 1887. He became a full partner in the firm (renamed Seward, Guthrie, & Morawetz) three years later at the age of thirty-one and was the lawyer of choice for investors in financial distressed railroads.[11]

It fell to Morawetz to put together the plan of reorganization for the AT&SF and oversee its implementation. Morawetz thought the divide between what was and what was not permissible was clear. He distinguished between two sorts of transactions. If a corporate debtor transferred assets to a new entity in a manner that undermined the rights of the existing creditors, then the existing creditors could reach the assets in the new corporation. On the other hand, if the assets were sold outright in good faith to a new entity, then the creditors of the old corporation could look only to the proceeds of the sale that the old corporation received.

---

[10] Robert T. Swaine, *The Cravath Firm and Its Predecessors: The Predecessor Firms 1819–1906* 382 (privately printed Ad Press, Ltd. 1946).

[11] See id., at 381–84.

Morawetz had an expansive view of what constituted good faith. In his view, cases such as *Howard* established only that the proceeds of a foreclosure sale could not be directed to the shareholders. Nothing prevented shareholders from enjoying a distribution from the senior committee once the senior committee acquired the railroad through its credit bid. From Morawetz's perspective, the principles of the Statute of 13 Elizabeth required the judge to do little policing of the senior committee that put together a plan of reorganization. The members of the senior committee were free to divide up ownership interests however they pleased as long as everything was done transparently and at arm's length.

It was not inherently objectionable if shareholders of the old corporation controlled the new one. It just required a little additional scrutiny: "[I]f the corporation receiving the transfer was controlled by the same persons as the company executing it, or if the real parties in interest in both companies were substantially the same, the burden of showing that the transfer was made in good faith, for value, would fall upon those asserting its validity against unpaid creditors."[12]

From Morawetz's perspective, the senior protective committee was a good faith purchaser. The old shareholders might end up controlling the new corporation, but this was completely permissible, as everything had been done openly and promoted the interests of creditors as a group.

Morawetz's position may not seem that much different from that of Lord Mansfield or even of the court in *Burd v. Smith*. But neither case raised the question of how much oversight was required when the relevant transaction took place as part of a legal process over which the court itself was presiding. The debtor in *Harman* made the transfer before the bankruptcy proceeding began. McClenachan could make an assignment for the benefit of creditors without going to court. Judges looked at the transaction only later. And the foreclosure action Gouverneur Morris instituted on Robert Morris's behalf also took place long before his bankruptcy. By contrast, the judge in an equity receivership was involved every step of the way. The relevant

[12] Victor Morawetz, *A Treatise on the Law of Private Corporations* §811 (Little, Brown 2d ed. 1886).

precedents did not speak to the kind of oversight that courts had to exercise over the processes that took place under their aegis.

Morawetz advanced the idea that once everything happened transparently and according to established practices, the oversight needed was quite modest. A court need not become involved – the principles of the Statute of 13 Elizabeth were not implicated – when an equity receivership was regularly conducted. As long as this was the case, the court could simply bless whatever plan emerged.

Accepting the reorganization plans was all the easier as the senior creditors usually agreed to share a large part of the railroad's value with those junior to them. They did not try to freeze out junior creditors as had been the case in *Howard*. Just before the receivership of the AT&SF began, the market's best guess of the value of the railroad was $125 million. Given that the senior creditors were owed $130 million at the time and controlled the process, it might seem that they could have taken the entire firm if they had wanted. For many today, this is the most puzzling feature of the equity receivership.

The representatives of the senior investors were investment bankers. The legal forms they used were just a vehicle for vindicating their norms. The investment bankers thought the implicit bargain among all the investors was to preserve the relative value of every investor's stake when a railroad needed a new capital structure. By their norms, a reorganization was just a substitute for an exchange offer. Just as the exchange offer maintained the value of each investor's stake in the railroad, the equity receivership did as well, at least for those who participated in it. It was not a day of reckoning akin to a cash sale or a liquidation. That the legal process took the form of sale was neither here nor there.

During this era, investment bankers had to return to the same investors again and again, and these investors inhabited every part of the capital structure.[13] Investors would not give them their capital for new projects if the bankers failed to distribute the stakes in reorganized railroads according to everyone's shared understanding that a restructuring was just an

---

[13] Carlos D. Ramirez, Did J. P. Morgan's Men Add Liquidity? Corporate Investment, Cash Flow, and Financial Structure at the Turn of the Twentieth Century, 50 *J. Fin.* 661, 664 (1995) (finding that Morgan's participation likely lowered the cost of capital).

exchange offer. It changed the capital structure of the railroad, but like the exchange offer, it did not change the relative value of each investor's stake.

Investment bankers of this era – and their lawyers – planned to be around for the long haul. Kidder Peabody survived until 1994. Another investment bank involved in the AT&SF reorganization, Barings, was founded in 1762 and survived until 1995. J. P. Morgan continues to flourish, as does Morawetz's law firm. If they violated the expectations of investors when they parceled out securities in reorganized firms, they would pay the price through the loss of future business.

The loyalties of these professionals went to the investors as a group, not to any particular constituency. Victor Morawetz's role in the AT&SF reorganization illustrates how surprisingly little of the reorganization involved battles between different investors over their stake in the firm. Morawetz was hired by a committee of junior bondholders in London to represent it in the reorganization, but this committee soon merged with the committee of senior bondholders. This joint committee then retained Morawetz to represent it, and he spearheaded the reorganization process as a whole.

None of the London bondholders complained when Morawetz started working for the senior bondholders as well as them. Also conspicuously missing from all the accounts of the reorganization are any complaints from the senior bondholders that in orchestrating the reorganization – including providing a substantial share of the reorganized business for the junior bondholders – Morawetz was working against them or had a conflict of interest.

No one thought there was a conflict because, under the distributional norms of the investment bankers, none existed. There was nothing problematic about the senior and junior bondholders forming a single committee and employing the same professionals in a world in which the railroad was going to continue operating. Indeed, none of the documents that set out the reorganization plan even identified which members of the committee were representing senior bondholders and which were representing junior ones.[14]

---

[14] See Plan and Agreement for the Reorganization of the Atchison, Topeka and Santa Fe Railroad Company, March 14, 1895.

These professionals had no interest in advancing the interests of one group at the expense of others. What mattered most to them was their reputation as faithful agents of all the investors in bad times as well as good. Their mission was to put the railroad on a sound footing in a fashion that promoted the interests of the investors as a group. They sought to act in a way that maximized the value of the business as a whole.

Moreover, the senior creditors did not have as large an incentive to resist distributions to junior investors as might first appear. In the first instance, distributing value to junior investors did not necessarily run contrary to the interest of the senior investors. In AT&SF and many other receiverships, many who held large senior positions in the capital structure held equally large junior positions at the same time. They were indifferent as to how ownership of the new railroad was carved up. From their perspective, any move that decreased the value of any one slice of their interest in the railroad necessarily increased another. Someone with a $100 senior bond and a $100 junior bond is indifferent between wiping out the junior bond and getting a new security worth $100 and, alternatively, including the junior bondholders and getting two securities back, one worth $67 and another worth $33.

Senior bondholders tolerated junior interests for another reason. Junior stakeholders could make nuisances of themselves if the senior creditors tried to exploit their legal entitlements to the limit. To be sure, it was unlikely that anyone during this period could make a cash bid that would top the credit bid of the senior creditors. But the junior bondholders might be able to argue that the railroad was worth more than the senior bondholders were owed and that they should be able to acquire ownership of the railroad subject to the lien of the senior bondholders. Indeed, early in the AT&SF receivership, exactly this course was contemplated. Only after some accounting scandals were uncovered did it become plain that the railroad was indeed worth less than what the senior creditors were owed.

The shareholders could have created difficulties as well. They could have pushed for an audit of the railroad's finances. They could have slowed down the process if they felt ignored without taking any steps that would generate the sort of badges of fraud that made Robert Morris and Blair McClenachan's conduct suspect. The railroad also needed additional cash to make needed capital investments, to pay for the costs of the reorganization, and to have something to pay the recalcitrant senior creditors who did not join the senior committee. Raising cash was hard. Firms that were being reorganized often had messy finances. Doing a new offering of shares and figuring out how to price them takes time. It is much easier to issue securities to existing shareholders in exchange for cash.

Including everyone in the reorganized firm was a way to minimize fights among the stakeholders. After all, such fights took attention away from what mattered most. The investors in the AT&SF needed to focus on solving the difficulties that their common debtor faced, and like most distressed debtors before and since, these difficulties were many. The AT&SF's chairman of the board died unexpectedly. In addition, the president had misled investors, and an outside audit showed that the railroad's earnings had been overstated. There was no evidence that any money had been siphoned away, but whatever credibility he had was gone. The president would have to be fired and a replacement found. Major operational issues remained.

A distressed railroad such as the AT&SF was like a ship in the middle of a storm, and the professionals running the railroad (including the managers, lawyers, and investment bankers) were captains of the ship. It made sense to preserve the value of the junior investors' stake so that they too would help see the ship through the storm. Preserving the value of each investor's stake in the firm gave everyone an incentive to focus on maximizing the value of the railroad. This was better than giving junior creditors an incentive to fight the reorganization, as they would if its effect was to wipe them out.

The restructured AT&SF emerged with two bond issues, preferred stock, and common stock. The bonds were given to the old senior bondholders, and they had a value roughly equal to that of the senior bonds just before the receivership began. The junior bondholders received preferred stock that traded for a value approximately equal to the value of the junior bonds at the time of the receivership, and the old shareholders retained their shares. Every stakeholder of a particular class was entitled to the same treatment as everyone else in the same class. The junior bondholders and the equityholders were required to shoulder the cost of reorganizing the railroad ($4 per bond and $10 per share respectively), but otherwise the reorganization itself did not change the value of the stake that the holders of the senior and junior bonds and the equityholders had.

On its face, the reorganization of the AT&SF seemed to leave all those with a stake in the railroad happy. As long as they participated in the reorganization, senior and junior bondholders as well as shareholders ended up with stakes in the new railroad that gave them the same relative share of the value of the firm they had before the reorganization. Trade creditors were paid in the ordinary course. Even though the foreclosure sale was a sale in form only, the receivership was nevertheless not a "fraud" on the rights of creditors. It did not undermine the rights of creditors as had been the case in *Burd v. Smith* or *Howard.*

There is, however, a significant qualification to the idea that the equity receivership simply replaced one capital structure with another and maintained the value of each investor's stake in the railroad. A railroad is not simply a stretch of track between two points. A railroad is a collection of lines that form a network. One of the major questions confronting a railroad that was being reorganized was whether to make changes in the network. Those running the process had to decide which lines to keep inside the firm and which ones to abandon.

The professionals charged with restructuring the AT&SF devoted much of their time to this question. The AT&SF leased a line in California that ran from Needles to Barstow, and it owned two other lines that connected Barstow with San Diego and Los Angeles respectively. The Atlantic & Pacific (A&P), a subsidiary of the AT&SF, connected these with the AT&SF's main line. The A&P consisted of a stretch of track between Albuquerque, New Mexico, and Needles, California. (Notwithstanding its name, the AT&SF's main line terminated in Albuquerque rather than in the more mountainous and less-accessible Santa Fe.) The A&P track allowed AT&SF to engage in transcontinental shipping, but this business was not nearly as lucrative as short-haul traffic. And if it wanted to engage in transcontinental shipping, the AT&SF could connect to the West Coast by leasing a line or entering into agreements with other carriers to carry goods the rest of the way from Albuquerque. In short, the investment bankers concluded that they did not need the A&P, nor did they need the help of its investors. The A&P (along with its investors) could be ignored.

This did not sit well with the bondholders of the A&P. And they enjoyed guarantees from the parent corporation, AT&SF. Hence, if the A&P proved unable to pay its bondholders in full outside of a receivership, A&P's bondholders had the ability to hold AT&SF liable for the entire debt of the subsidiary. Once the receivership started, however, the norms of the investment bankers did not require them to give the A&P bondholders a stake in the reorganized railroad.

The guarantee that the A&P bondholders enjoyed made them creditors of the parent, but they were only general creditors. They enjoyed no priority. Because the amount bid at the receivership sale of the AT&SF was less than what the senior creditors were owed, the A&P bondholders were not, as a formal legal matter, entitled to any of the proceeds from the foreclosure sale. And the norms of the investment bankers provided that only those investors whose lines remained part of the network were entitled to a piece of the reorganized firm. Hence, the A&P bondholders were left with nothing even though they held guarantees against the parent corporation and, as a legal matter, stood in a position superior to that of the AT&SF shareholders. The A&P was not part of the AT&SF's future. Its bondholders found themselves in the same storm, but, as far as the investment bankers were concerned, they were on a different ship.

The A&P bondholders tried to argue that the court should not approve a plan that siphoned value from the senior bondholders to the old equityholders. The A&P bondholders invoked the same principles that the creditors of Blair McClenachan invoked in *Burd v. Smith* and the general creditors of the railroad invoked in *Howard*. As with other equity receiverships during this period, however, the creditors of the A&P lost this argument. Courts deferred to the investment bankers and other professionals when they decided whether a particular creditor was entitled to participate in the reorganization.

Morawetz, while representing J. P. Morgan, prevailed on exactly this issue in another equity receivership a year later.[15] The appellate

---

[15] Morawetz shared the laboring oar in this appeal with Francis Stetson, another great lawyer of the era. Stetson's law firm, now called Davis Polk, still flourishes, and J. P. Morgan remains one of its important clients.

court found that there was nothing objectionable about a reorganization plan "unless it can be said that it was a scheme to defraud creditors."[16] As the court explained:

> [I]t is suggested by [the junior creditors] that, upon any plan of reorganization, the parties in interest are not to be at liberty to contract with each other; but that the plan of reorganization should be formulated and imposed upon the parties by a court of equity. Courts are created for the purpose of enforcing contracts which parties have made, not for the purpose of making contracts for parties. It would be more than doubtful, if power was conferred upon a court to make a contract for parties, whether it could make as fair and just and equitable a contract as could the parties themselves.[17]

Under this view, a restructuring is "fair and just and equitable" if it reflects a bargain struck among the stakeholders conducted according to whatever customs constrain the parties. Judges supervise the reorganization, but judges do not dictate the outcome of the bargaining among sophisticated parties. The court does not intervene as long as there is nothing underhanded about the way the plan is forged. Among other things, the court is simply not competent to craft details of a plan of reorganization. In an equity receivership, investment bankers and other professionals did the heavy lifting. As they had the incentive to do right by the stakeholders as a group, it made sense to give them a loose rein.

The plan that emerged in the AT&SF reorganization did not have any of the tell-tale signs that made McClenachan's or Morris's transactions suspect. The AT&SF transaction was designed to restore the railroad to sound financial health. In forging this transaction, the investment bankers and professionals like Morawetz exercised their best judgment about the sensible boundaries of the firm going forward. As long as they did this, the court respected their bargain.

That the A&P bondholders had legal rights against the railroad before the receivership began was neither here nor there. As a legal matter, their rights as junior bondholders were extinguished by the

---

[16] Paton v. Northern Pacific Railroad Co., 85 F. 838, 842 (C.C.E.D. Wis. 1896).
[17] 85 F at 843.

foreclosure sale. Hence, they could expect to receive only what the norms of the investment bankers gave them. And as far as the norms of the investment bankers were concerned, the A&P was not part of the firm on a going-forward basis. Hence, its bondholders were not entitled to share in the value of the reorganized firm. As Morawetz conceived the equity receivership, the oversight that the judge provided in the reorganization bargain should be modest. If investment bankers and lawyers adhered to their norms, there was nothing for the court to do.

Just a few years after the reorganization of the AT&SF, however, the Supreme Court sounded a different note. The receivership of the Louisville, New Albany, and Chicago Railway Company, commonly known as the Monon, came before the Supreme Court.[18] The railway had guaranteed bonds of a subsidiary, as the AT&SF had guaranteed the A&P's. The bondholders of the subsidiary sought to hold the parent to the guarantee, but before they could vindicate their rights in court, the railway persuaded a general creditor to put it into receivership. There was a foreclosure sale, and as in the reorganization of the AT&SF, the claims of the bondholders on their guarantee were wiped out.

When the case reached it, the Supreme Court held that the lower court should not have allowed the receivership to go forward. Courts had to exercise serious oversight in every restructuring. The Supreme Court remanded to the lower court to see if the receivership was a scheme to defeat the rights of general creditors. The lower court had not given the railway's reorganization plan the kind of scrutiny that was required. In its view, a court could "never rightfully become the mere silent registrar of the agreements."[19]

Once judges were called upon to oversee a receivership, they cannot be idle spectators. Courts had to ensure that the receivership is not part of a scheme to hinder, delay, or defraud creditors. Judges must draw a distinction between the right of the senior bondholder "who has acquired absolute title by foreclosure to mortgaged property to thereafter give of his interest to others" and an illegitimate attempt on the part of the senior bondholder "to destroy the interest of all unsecured

---

[18] See Louisville Trust Co. v. Louisville, New Albany & Chicago Railway Co., 174 U.S. 674 (1899).

[19] 174 U.S. at 688.

creditors, to secure a waiver of all objections on the part of the stock-holder, and consummate speedily the foreclosure."[20]

Some of the language in *Monon* suggested that general creditors could not be wiped out if equityholders received something in a reorganization. But a better reading of the case is that the judge must attend to the process itself, not the substance of bargains that the parties reached. What mattered was not what each stakeholder received, but whether the process was indeed one that served to advance the interests of the investors as a group. The Monon went through the receivership only because it was trying to thwart its bond-holders. In that sense, it was no different from what the debtor attempted in *Burd v. Smith*. A transfer, even to a completely legitimate creditor, can be struck down if the purpose of the transaction is to thwart the rights of other creditors.

Morawetz downplayed the importance of *Monon*. He believed that nothing the Supreme Court said was inconsistent with what he had said in his treatise. Transactions that did not advance legitimate economic aims, but rather promoted the interests of some at the expense of others could be struck down. In *Monon*, the owners of the railroad instituted the receivership for the purpose of extinguishing a guarantee, just as McClenachan assigned his property as part of an effort to thwart some of his creditors. The equity receivership of the AT&SF was cut from a different cloth altogether. The AT&SF receivership would have happened even if there had been no A&P bondholders. The treatment of the A&P bondholders was a consequence of charting the best course for the railroad going forward.

In the case of the AT&SF, those in control of the reorganization decided that, as a sound business matter, a particular stretch of track did not belong inside the firm. Once they made this decision, they did not have to give a seat at the bargaining table to those who invested in that track. As long as the realities of the business drove decision-making in a receivership, the court should not interfere. The equitable prin-ciples that the judge relied upon to police the proceeding were not implicated.

[20] 174 U.S. at 688.

For Morawetz, the Court in *Monon* was asking only for courts to give greater scrutiny to each reorganization than had been the practice, but reorganizations such as that of the AT&SF still passed muster. It was one thing to insist on giving the reorganization process greater scrutiny to ensure that it was not a scheme to deprive creditors of their rights and quite another to intrude into responsible decision-making by investment bankers and other professionals.

But it was possible to read *Monon* more broadly than Morawetz did. Under this reading, the Supreme Court held that courts were not to give a pass card to a reorganization simply because it is being run by professionals honestly intent upon preserving the business. The principle at work in *Burd v. Smith* as applied to reorganizations requires a hard look at the process. As the Court explained:

> No such receivership can be initiated and carried on unless absolutely subject to the independent judgment of the court ... and [the] court in the administration of such receivership ... must see to it that all equitable rights in or connected with the property are secured.[21]

In particular, the court must ensure that each stakeholder has a chance to negotiate on equal terms.

The Supreme Court revisited this issue again in 1913 in *Northern Pacific Railway Co. v. Boyd.*[22] It was reviewing the same reorganization in which Morawetz had previously prevailed in *Paton*. On its face, the case was much weaker. The creditor who brought the appeal took more than a decade to establish his claim.[23] Rather than an investor in the enterprise, he had supplied services to a spur line. More to the point, the reorganization had been regularly conducted, the assets had been found insufficient to pay the senior creditors in full, and none of the value that the secured creditors chose to give to the old shareholders was tainted with any badge of fraud.

The Court nevertheless found fault with the way the receivership was conducted. It did not deny that the senior creditors could do with

---

[21] 174 U.S. at 689.
[22] Northern Pacific Railway Co. v. Boyd, 228 U.S. 482 (1913).
[23] Morawetz had retired by the time *Boyd* came to the Supreme Court, and Stetson argued the case without his help.

their share in the railroad what they pleased, but the legal process was what established this share in the first place. The foreclosure sale, as everyone knew, was just a legal device to allow bargaining to take place under a judicial umbrella. One could not rely on such a mechanism to extinguish a creditor's rights if that creditor was never invited to participate in the reorganization. Square corners had to be cut.

To be sure, this creditor would have had nothing to complain about if the senior stakeholders had simply gone about exercising their rights. But once they drew equityholders into the negotiations, the court had to ensure that no one exploited their control over the process to their own advantage at the expense of the general creditors. As soon as the senior creditors struck a deal with the shareholders, they lost the ability to ignore the interests of the general creditors. It was not enough for those participating in the reorganization process to have good intentions. They had to include everyone in the bargaining process.

If *Boyd* had been handed down before the AT&SF was reorganized, the A&P bondholders would have had to be included in plan negotiations. Their guarantees made them creditors of the parent company, and this alone was enough to entitle them to participate in the reorganization.

The principle that the court invoked against McClenachan had evolved. It was no longer sufficient that the motive behind the transaction was benign. In order for a court to bless a transaction that altered the rights of creditors, the affected creditors had to be included in the process. The Court stopped short of insisting that the general creditors receive any particular distribution. They received only whatever emerged from the bargaining process. As the Court explained, "If [a general creditor] declines a fair offer he is left to protect himself as any other creditor of a judgment debtor, and, having refused to come into a just reorganization, could not thereafter be heard in a court of equity to attack it."[24]

Boyd is another link in the chain of cases that connects the sort of oversight that a judge must give to a reorganization to the Statute of 13 Elizabeth. Morawetz had believed that the principles that derived from the Statute of 13 Elizabeth merely required the court to ensure that

[24] Northern Pacific Railway Co. v. Boyd, 228 U.S. 482, 508 (1913).

those engaged in the plan formation process were not intentionally undermining the rights of other creditors. After *Boyd*, it became clear that this was not enough. A judge supervising a reorganization had an affirmative obligation to ensure that everyone had a fair opportunity to participate in the process. Judges could not assume that professionals would themselves reach a deal that was "fair and just and equitable." Judges themselves had an obligation to police the process to ensure that it was "fair and just and equitable."

The Supreme Court in *Boyd* left open the question of what it meant to participate in the bargaining process and be given a fair offer. It said comparatively little about how the judge should go about policing the behavior of the parties to the negotiations. Nevertheless, by this time the principles that animate the Statute of 13 Elizabeth had expanded significantly. There is no longer any doubt that the focus looks at the process as a whole and not discrete transfers by the debtor. Someone like Morris would not be able to argue that the annuity the Dutch investors promised to give his wife was immune from scrutiny merely because it did not involve any transfer of property by him. Moreover, care has to be taken to ensure that no one is shut out. The entire proceeding, seen in its totality, has to be done in a way that does not "hinder, delay, or defraud" or, to say the same thing, is "fair and just and equitable."

To return to *Howard*, after *Boyd* it no longer mattered whether the buyer of the railroad was to give part of the consideration directly to the shareholders of the old corporation. Any process in which value ended up in the old shareholders' hands, however indirect, was suspect. Senior creditors cannot vindicate their rights in a process that pays too little attention to the rights of the other creditors. Side deals that corrupt or even cloud the process are forbidden.

Morawetz had been comfortable with a judge providing only loose oversight, and it is exactly this conception of the underlying principles of corporate reorganization that *Boyd* rejected. The reorganization of the AT&SF might well have slighted the rights of the bondholders of the A&P. Indeed, later events suggest as much. The A&P itself went into receivership, and the reorganized AT&SF appeared at the fore-closure sale and acquired the track between Albuquerque and Needles. In the end, the AT&SF was able to keep the assets of the A&P and exclude its bondholders from sharing in the value they brought to the business.

By the start of the twentieth century, the Supreme Court had extended fraudulent conveyance principles well beyond the idea that courts could strike down transactions, even if regular in form, in which there was suspect behavior by a Robert Morris or shareholders like those in *Howard*. Courts went beyond blessing agreements merely because creditors struck a bargain among themselves in good faith. They ensured that the bargaining that led to such an agreement was inclusive and the process fair.

This transformation of the core principle governing debtor-creditor relations came with the risk that reorganizations would become more expensive and less likely to succeed. The AT&SF reorganization, notwithstanding the short shrift given to the A&P bondholders, was a spectacular success. The reorganization plan issued long-term bonds when the railroad emerged from reorganization in 1895, and these were paid off in full and on time exactly one hundred years later, in 1995. The AT&SF, now part of the BNSF, continues to flourish. None of this might have happened with a longer or more contentious reorganization.

The change in the law brought by *Boyd* had no direct effect on the fortunes of Victor Morawetz, however. His career as a lawyer overseeing reorganizations was short. He left his law firm to become the general counsel of the AT&SF and soon became chairman of its board. Through his investments in the railroad, Morawetz became rich and retired young. During retirement he lived well, wrote about the law and law reform, and, with Elihu Root, founded the American Law Institute.

Morawetz's firm continued to represent the AT&SF and its successor and does so to the present day. Of course, the firm had to find a new partner to replace Morawetz, but an able associate in the office was promoted and rose to the challenge. Within a few years, this lawyer became head of the firm. He put his own mark on reorganization law, as did another lawyer he recruited out of law school, who was soon made a partner as well. Their names were Paul Cravath and Robert Swaine respectively.

Equity receiverships were effective in large part because the professionals had a powerful incentive to do right by investors throughout the capital structure. They intended to be around for the long term and knew that they would encounter these investors again. I once pressed a partner at Morawetz's firm about Morawetz's representation of the AT&SF and the apparent conflict that arose from his representation of creditors in multiple layers of capital structure at the same time. He had only admiration for the work that Morawetz had done during the AT&SF receivership,[25] but he refused to discuss the particulars of Morawetz's apparent conflict of interest. He explained that he was bound by the attorney-client privilege. That all of this had happened more than a century before was neither here nor there. Lawyers at this firm do not disclose client confidences, no matter how much time has passed.

As the principles of the Statute of 13 Elizabeth expanded in the domain of equity receiverships, they were also being reshaped in another sphere. The focus there was on a different sort of debtor and a different sort of harm to creditors. The next chapter turns to this arena.

---

[25] The familiarity of this lawyer with the particulars of the AT&SF reorganization was not unusual. Rarely does a debate among reorganization lawyers not lead sooner or later to a discussion of nineteenth-century railroads.

3 THE CREDIT MEN

Although the Supreme Court expanded the oversight that judges had to give to equity receiverships, investment bankers still retained largely a free hand in sorting out the rights of a distressed railroad. The judge was under no obligation to assess the substance of the bargain struck between the parties. If the negotiations passed muster, the bargains were enforced according to their terms. Beyond ensuring that deals were struck honestly and in good faith, courts did not interfere. The investment bankers were in control. The positions they held on the boards ensured that creditors from outside their circle could not derail the reorganization and that debtors could not commandeer it.

A push for greater oversight, however, did arise elsewhere. Here a handful of dissenting creditors had the ability to thwart legitimate efforts of the majority to restructure debt. The question became whether the principles of the Statute of 13 Elizabeth could be reshaped to protect creditors as a group against a small minority who undermined their efforts.

Over the last several decades of the nineteenth century and the first few decades of the twentieth, a new set of players emerged who had to sort out the affairs of a different sort of distressed debtor. The growth of railroads in the nineteenth century, in addition to facilitating the shipment of agricultural products to the east, dramatically expanded the flow of goods in the other direction. Wholesalers and manufacturers shipped goods all across the country. Their customers were small retailers. The retailers acquired goods on credit and repaid when their own customers paid them. By the end of the nineteenth century, the amount of trade credit approached $15 billion when the total amount of money in circulation was only $1 billion.[1] Most retailers paid their debts in full, but some did not and, when they did not, creditors faced a new challenge.

Wholesalers and manufacturers lived hundreds of miles from each other and from their retail merchant debtors.[2] Distance alone created challenges radically different from those that came before. Robert Morris's creditors dealt with him face to face and put him in debtor's prison when he defaulted. Investors in the AT&SF had investment bankers who could watch over the board and start an equity receivership when things went south.

By virtue of being remote and scattered from each other, creditors of distant retailers had only a limited ability to vindicate their rights in court. Even when they could navigate the idiosyncratic procedures of a faraway venue, these procedures heavily favored local creditors. And even if the procedures had been scrupulously fair, ordinary debt collection was a race that went to the swift, and local creditors typically could reach whatever assets a debtor had long before a distant wholesaler could.

Those who pursued distant retail merchants differed from earlier merchants along another important dimension as well. During the time of Robert Morris, a single merchant would both make the sale and decide whether to extend credit. By the end of the nineteenth century, the large wholesalers relied on a new managerial class that oversaw the operations of the company. And among these managers were those who focused exclusively on credit. They did not think of themselves as being experts in the dry goods business or in the hardware business, but in finance. They saw themselves as professionals, much like lawyers, investment bankers, or doctors. They called themselves credit men.[3]

---

[1] These figures are based on the estimates of Lyman George, President McKinley's secretary of the treasury. See Lyman J. George, "American Enterprise – Some of Its Trials and Achievements," *The Lawyer and Credit Men* 8 (May 1898), quoted in David Sellers Smith, The Elimination of the Unworthy: Credit Men and Small Retailers in Progressive Era Capitalism, 9 *Journal of the Gilded Age and Progressive Era* 197, 207 (2010).

[2] Bradley Hansen, Commercial Associations and the Creation of a National Economy: The Demand for Federal Bankruptcy Law, 72 *Business History Rev.* 86, 92 (1998).

[3] For a history of the National Association of Credit Men, see J. Harry Tregoe, Pioneers and Traditions of the National Association of Credit Men, in *Souvenir Program, Golden Anniversary* (National Association of Credit Men 1947).

Initially, each credit man relied on his own ability to review a borrower's creditworthiness, gather whatever intelligence he needed to make a credit decision, and then use his own resources and ingenuity to recover what he could when things went badly. But in the wake of the Panic of 1893, many credit men recognized that they would benefit from acting collectively.[4]

The Panic of 1893, the same economic depression that triggered the receivership of the Atchison, Topeka, and Santa Fe, brought on the failure of many retail merchants. A group of credit men first gathered at the Columbian Exposition in Chicago in 1894. Two years later, a larger group gathered in Toledo and formed the National Association of Credit Men. The credit men believed in improving the methods of gathering and disseminating credit information, as well as adopting "new laws beneficial to commerce" and reforming those that were "unfavorable to honest debtors and creditors."[5] Their ranks swelled to 33,000 by 1920.[6]

By organizing, the credit men could more easily exchange information among themselves. In addition, organizing allowed them to pool resources and maintain tighter control of their debtors. After the credit men joined forces, they established local adjustment bureaus in every major city and many smaller ones. The people who ran these bureaus helped dispersed credit men to act as one and navigate together the challenges they faced in remote places when one of their debtors failed to pay.

Typical was Henry Hirshberg, who headed the bureau in San Antonio. He was a lawyer who also led the local chamber of commerce. Active in local politics, Hirshberg was a force for good government who worked to defeat machine candidates. Hirshberg later became an avid supporter of the New Deal.

Among other things, Hirshberg would come to know Lyndon Johnson. Indeed, when Johnson impetuously decided to marry Lady Bird without giving advance notice to anyone (not even to Lady Bird), he turned to Hirshberg for help. Johnson had decided to have the

---

[4] See Smith, supra note 1, at 197.

[5] Peter P. Wahlstad, *Credit and the Credit Man* 222 (Alexander Hamilton Institute 1917).

[6] See Rowena Olegario, *A Culture of Credit: Embedding Trust and Transparency in American Business* 176 (Harvard University Press 2006).

wedding in San Antonio, and he called on Hirshberg after he was already en route. Johnson told Hirshberg to make the wedding arrangements that day, serve as best man, and host a dinner that same evening at a local hotel. Hirshberg made it all happen. He even had enough pull with the hotel management to be allowed to bring several bottles of his own sparkling burgundy to the dinner, even though San Antonio was dry at the time.[7]

As this later adventure illustrates, Hirshberg was someone who could exercise initiative and serve as a loyal agent at the same time. The credit men chose people like Hirshberg to represent them. The credit men stood to gain when those they picked to run the local adjustment bureaus were respectable members of the local community. Such a person was well positioned to identify honest and able merchants and distinguish them from those who engaged in sharp practices. With someone like Henry Hirshberg there to represent them, the credit men were able to assess their debtor and make the best of a bad situation. Hirshberg allowed the credit men to act collectively even when they were far from San Antonio and from each other. Other forces bonded the credit men together as well.

The National Association had an annual convention and produced a journal that included both trade information and inspirational articles. Credit men also formed local associations. Each city's association met regularly. The group celebrated in the same fashion as other fraternal organizations before and since. Credit men found common cause because their work together advanced the economic interests of the firm that employed each of them. By working together, each could identify better credit risks and recover more from those who defaulted. But once they were organized and met regularly, the fact of coming together and articulating their mission led them to form common bonds. The ideals they embraced took on a life of their own.

At the first annual meeting of the New York Credit Men's Association in April 1897, more than 150 gathered at the St. Denis Hotel.[8] The tables were decorated with lilies, roses, and tulips, and a Hungarian band played. Once cigars were lit, the secretary of the

---

[7] See Henry Hirshberg, Lyndon Baines Johnson Library Oral History Collection, October 17, 1968, at 7–10.
[8] The Credit Men's Dinner, N.Y. Times, April 23, 1897, at 2.

National Association described what the group was about: "There is no class of men more industrious, efficient, and responsible than the credit men. On their shoulders rests the burden of all the credit of this country, and the financial success of thousands of mercantile industries entrusted to their keeping."

Then a few politicians stood up and told bad jokes. For the rest of the evening, credit men took turns offering testimonials to their profession. The New York Credit Men's president addressed the group:

> The creditor no longer owns the debtor in law or in fact. The former now shares in the good or bad fortune of the latter; all that he asks is that there shall be no fraudulent conversion of the assets in the case of failure. Rarely, indeed, can be found a case where there is no fraud in failure that a majority of creditors are not willing to accept a dividend and leave to the debtor something with which to start again.

Credit men embodied the spirit of progressivism. It was their professional duty to ensure that credit was parceled out and collected in a way that was consistent with the highest standards. Like the members of other associations formed during the Progressive Era, the credit men shared what Robert Wiebe has called "a passionate concern for moral capitalism."[9] By ensuring that credit flowed only to worthy debtors, they protected the economy from the excesses of laissez-faire. The credit men took pride in the noble activity in which they were engaged.

The credit men lived in a world in which the strong norms they developed among themselves allowed them to cooperate with each other even though they were dispersed, and the law had little to offer them. Their code of conduct was consistent with their economic interests, but it was deeply held. They divided their debtors into two types: the unworthy and the worthy. Unworthy debtors were those who were less than straight. Once identified, the credit men would have them prosecuted if they could, but usually they could do no more than cut them off. They would collect what little they could and move on. Their best defense against the unworthy was constant vigilance.

But there were also the worthy debtors. These were those who, though they fell into trouble, were competent and forthright. When

---

[9] Robert H. Wiebe, *Businessmen and Reform: A Study of the Progressive Movement* 9 (Harvard University Press 1962).

they defaulted, it was a consequence of misfortune, and they deserved sympathy. It was possible to sort things out without resort to legal process. The sensible path, when the debtor was honest and able, was voluntary forbearance on the part of everyone. Credit men as a group would allow honest debtors to sell off their stock over time and pay everyone a part of what they owed. These were called "friendly adjustments." The credit men believed their interests were best served when each of the creditors cooperated with one another. As long as no one jumped the gun, there would be a decent chance that everyone would be paid as much as circumstances permitted. Having sympathy for the honest but unlucky debtor, in addition to being honorable and upright, was also good business.

This distinction between the unworthy and the worthy was expressed in the third principle set out in the *Canons of Commercial Ethics*, the aspirational values credit men promoted at their dinners and promulgated in their trade journal: "To punish and expose the guilty is one thing; to help the unfortunate but innocent debtor to rise is another; but both duties are equally important, for both duties make for a higher moral standard of action on the part of business men."[10]

During this era, the credit men rarely noticed or cared whether their debtor enjoyed limited liability. They had the choice of extending terms, shutting the business down and selling off its stock, or agreeing to take a reduced payment in return for a release. In assessing these options, the form in which the retailer did business did not matter. Rarely could one of these retail businesses stand on its own when separated from the person who owned and ran it. Without the entrepreneur, the only assets were inventory and accounts receivable. To be sure, it was possible in theory to hold the small, unincorporated retail debtor personally liable for the debts of the business, but this was usually a waste of time. Homestead and other exemptions available under state law protected primarily the assets of the households of individual debtors. The credit men rarely looked to nonbusiness assets in making their original extensions of credit.

---

[10] Canons of Commercial Ethics Adopted by the National Association of Credit Men, reprinted in The Ethics of the Professions and of Business, 101 *Annals of the American Academy of Political and Social Science* 298–300 (May 1922).

The focus of the credit men was on how debtors used the credit extended to them in their business. As a manual of the period explained:

> It is sufficient to point out that no man is blameless who diverts to his own use funds belonging to another. Even tho such a dealer has no deliberate purpose to defraud his creditors, he is nevertheless unworthy of consideration as proper credit risk. His business does not "owe him a living" unless he actually earns it. When this "living" has to come out of the creditors' capital, the boundaries of business integrity are clearly being overstepped.[11]

Credit men would not compromise their firm's claims if they thought their debtors were conning them or even being less than completely forthright. But if distressed merchants were utterly transparent and willing to pay what they could, it was in the interest of credit men to stay their hands and work with one another to give these debtors a chance to pay back part of what they owed. According to the ninth canon in the *Canons of Commercial Ethics*: "[I]t is uncooperative and commercially unethical for a creditor to refuse the friendly instrument or the composition arbitrarily and force thereby a form of administration that will be prejudicial and expensive to the interest of everyone concerned."[12]

In contrast to the investment bankers who could call upon federal judges to help them sort out the affairs of distressed railroads, the credit men found themselves in a desolate legal environment. The equity receivership that proved so useful in the case of an insolvent railroad was of little use to them. Their debtors were too small to justify such an elaborate procedure, and the businesses had no value apart from those who owned and operated them.

In theory, the credit men could call upon ordinary methods of debt collection in local courts, but it was hard to take advantage of them at a distance. Moreover, invoking legal procedures was usually counterproductive. Long before they could realize on any assets, local creditors would have seized all there was.

Against this backdrop, the credit men attempted to use the legal system to hold unworthy debtors to account. The credit men devoted

[11] Peter P. Wahlstad, supra note 5, at 64.
[12] Canon No. 9, supra note 10, at 299.

considerable time to promoting state laws that criminalized false reporting to credit agencies.[13] The credit men also took the lead in promoting the passage of bulk sales laws. These focused on a particular type of fraud, one that occurred when a retailer sold its entire inventory, all acquired on credit, to someone who passed as a good faith purchaser, and then skipped town. The credit men also tried to strengthen the enforcement of existing laws against fraud. They established their own Investigation and Prosecution Bureau, eventually spending millions of dollars to develop tight relations with local authorities. These efforts led to hundreds of convictions.[14]

Of interest to us are the efforts of the credit men to strengthen their hand in dealing with worthy debtors. The credit men wanted legal reforms that made it easier for them to reach a sensible accommodation with worthy debtors. Friendly adjustments worked only if all the creditors were willing to stay their hand. The norms of the credit men kept them from gun-jumping. It was harder, however, to persuade creditors who lived close to the debtor to forbear. These included small banks as well as friends and associates who lent money to the debtor. Among other things, these creditors had greater access to the local courts. More to the point, they were not part of the credit men's fraternity. The credit men therefore pursued legal reforms that would push these local creditors towards cooperating with them.

The credit men directed their attention to the federal government and its power to enact uniform laws on the subject of bankruptcies. Until the late nineteenth century, the few bankruptcy laws that Congress passed had only brief and unsuccessful lives, and they were focused on debtor misbehavior, such as hiding assets or themselves from the reach of creditors. These bankruptcy laws were aimed at empowering creditors when ordinary methods of debt collection failed. They provided a mechanism that forced the debtor to gather assets and distribute them. In practice, however, these laws yielded creditors little and shed even less light on the debtor's affairs.

---

[13] A quarter of the states had passed such laws by 1915. David Sellers Smith, The Elimination of the Unworthy: Credit Men and Small Retailers in Progressive Era Capitalism, 9 *Journal of the Gilded Age and Progressive Era* 197, 216 (2010).
[14] See id., at 217.

The bankruptcy laws of 1841 and 1867 had been passed in response to financial depressions, had worked poorly, and had been quickly repealed.[15] The credit men, however, believed that a new bankruptcy law could help them over a rather different dimension. Instead of seeing bankruptcy as a forum that would help them recover assets, they saw it as a device that would deter unworthy debtors and check misbehavior on the part of local creditors. Such a law would create the space they needed to make the most of a bad situation. The credit men spent considerable time and energy during the 1880s and 1890s lobbying Congress for bankruptcy legislation.[16] They finally succeeded in 1898, when Republicans controlled the House of Representatives, the Senate, and the White House.[17]

This new iteration of bankruptcy law limited the freedom of creditors in advance of bankruptcy. This was a dramatic break with the past. It had long been common ground that individual creditors were entitled to pursue their debtors before the bankruptcy began. There was nothing wrong with individual creditors taking advantage of every avenue of recovery available to them, even when bankruptcy was imminent. Individual creditors were empowered to sue and recover from an uncooperative debtor, and preference law did nothing to stop them.

The vice of the preference that Lord Mansfield identified in *Harman v. Fishar* was bad behavior on the part of the debtor. The original focus of preference law was entirely on debtors and whether they had done anything to thwart creditors – such as remaining at home and thus insulating themselves from legal process or concealing their goods to prevent creditors from taking them in execution. The essence of a preference was that the debtor was picking and choosing among creditors even as bankruptcy was in prospect. In the absence of bad behavior by a debtor, a preference could not exist.

[15] Act of August 19, 1841, ch. 9, 5 Stat. 440 (repealed 1843); Act of March 2, 1867, ch. 176, 14 Stat. 517 (repealed 1878).
[16] See Bradley Hansen, Commercial Associations and the Creation of a National Economy: The Demand for Federal Bankruptcy Law, 72 *Business History Rev.* 86–113 (Spring 1998).
[17] Act of July 1, 1898, ch. 541, 30 Stat. 544. For the definitive account of the political forces that led to each of this country's bankruptcy laws, see David A. Skeel, Jr., *Debt's Dominion: A History of Bankruptcy Law in America* (Princeton University Press 2001).

The credit men did not share this view that an individual creditor was free to pursue a distressed debtor without regard for other creditors. Nor did they view courts as particularly helpful to them in their efforts to recover assets. The credit men could coordinate actions among themselves without the help of the law. Legal proceedings were much more expensive than their own "friendly adjustments."[18] For these two reasons, the credit men saw bankruptcy law not as a mechanism to collect debt, but rather as a device that would put a stop to anything that undercut their efforts to work together outside of formal legal proceedings.

The 1898 Bankruptcy Act did leave in place state homestead and other exemption laws that put a significant portion of a debtor's assets beyond the creditor's reach. The credit men did not like such laws, but they lacked the political muscle to do much about them. Instead, the 1898 Act was designed with the specific aim of keeping local creditors from acting precipitously.[19] For the credit men, bankruptcy law acted in the first instance as a trip wire, a deterrent that preserved a space in which they could engage in informal negotiations with their debtor.

The 1898 Act, from the perspective of the credit men, was largely about deterring bad behavior. There was one respect, however, in which the 1898 Act affirmatively helped creditors act collectively. It allowed for "compositions." Compositions served a purpose parallel to the equity receivership. They provided a way to overcome a collective action problem if an informal bargain among the creditors was not possible. When a large majority of creditors agreed to accept a certain number of cents on the dollar, dissenting creditors could be bound. A majority could act on behalf of the creditors as a whole.

The credit men were wary of legal mechanisms that displaced their own efforts to bring about consensus. They acknowledged legal

---

[18] See Thomas Clifford Billig, What Price Bankruptcy: A Plea for "Friendly Adjustment," 14 *Cornell L. Rev.* 413, 429 (1929).

[19] Others have made this observation. See, e.g., Robert Weisberg, Commercial Morality, the Merchant Character, and the History of the Voidable Preference, 39 *Stan. L. Rev.* 3, 4 (1986). ("As American bankruptcy law evolved from the English model at the start of the nineteenth century, the law of preferential transfers shifted its concern from the culpability of the debtor to the culpability of the favored creditor. It thus sought to discourage, if not punish, aggressive self-interested economic behavior by imposing on individual creditors a social or moral duty to their fellow creditors.")

coercion might overcome lone dissenters, but they worried as much about how it might be abused. They feared that the debtor and a few local creditors could commandeer the process. Unless they could ensure the active participation by all the credit men, they might be outvoted and left with less than they would have if left to their own devices.

For this reason, a composition was far from the credit men's first choice. It came into play only when attempts at a voluntary workout had failed. A composition might be useful, but it depended upon the debtor and the creditor actively cooperating with one another. From the perspective of the credit men, courts had to ensure that the bargain reached reflected the interests of the creditors as a group. It was not enough merely to review for bad faith or ensure that everyone had a seat at the table. Even if there was no obvious misbehavior and even if the explicit rules were followed, the bargain reached might not have been a sensible one. If it failed to advance the interests of the creditors as a group, the judge should not allow it to go forward.

The dynamics at work could produce a composition that did not reflect the collective interests of the creditors. A debtor might make a low-ball offer to the creditors as a group, and most of them might decide to take what they were offered rather than press for more. It was costly to turn down a debtor's offer and pursue distant remedies. Each creditor was tempted to acquiesce. As one credit man explained, "The first thing we think when a man offers fifty cents on the dollar is 'take it, I can't afford to be bothered anymore.' "[20] The credit men wanted the court to put a stop to such compositions even if the debtor were able to round up enough votes from creditors who did not adhere to their principles.

The 1898 Act required the judge to find that the composition was in "the best interests of the creditors."[21] This was the lever that the credit men counted upon to ensure that courts gave composition agreements a hard look. A review of the dynamics in the case that led to the modern understanding of "best interests" provides a window on how the test developed and how it fell short.

---

[20] Lee M. Hutchins, Fraudulent Failures, Bulletin of the National Association of Credit Men, January 1916, pp. 9, 11.

[21] 30 Stat. at 550.

Saul Wolfson Dry Goods was one of the oldest businesses in San Antonio. Saul Wolfson himself was born in Germany in 1830. He began working in his uncle's wood business before emigrating to the United States in the 1850s. He joined the army at the start of the Civil War, fought at the First Battle of Bull Run, and served until the end of the war.

Like others of the time, Saul Wolfson went west to make his fortune. With the help of his brother, he opened a dry goods business in San Antonio. The forerunner of the modern department store, a dry goods store sold textiles, dresses, and sundries. When Wolfson started, he operated out of a single room. The business grew over time, and eventually Wolfson was selling everything from men's suits and hats to shoes, women's dresses, carpeting, and furniture.

As the business expanded, Wolfson became wealthy. He moved into a substantial Victorian mansion. He became a familiar figure in San Antonio. He could be seen every day taking the ten-minute walk from his home to his store at the center of town. He was a natural salesman, known for "his cheery, happy manner and his never-failing courtesy to all."[22]

At the same time that Marshall Field became known for "giving the lady what she wants" and Harry Selfridge for telling his employees that "the customer is always right," Saul Wolfson promised his customers "a square deal." He had moved early to charging all customers the same price and freeing them from the burden of haggling over price. He incentivized his workers by giving them a percentage of the revenues they generated over and above their salary once their sales in any pay period exceeded a given level.

Wolfson occupied a substantial building at the corner of Alamo and Commerce. He maintained a full-time buyer in New York. Each department had a buyer who spent as much time in eastern markets as in the store. There were affiliations with manufacturers on the East Coast and abroad. By the time Saul Wolfson celebrated his fiftieth anniversary in business, he was a prominent citizen in San Antonio, recognized for his "unostentatious philanthropy."

---

[22] See Firm Celebrates Golden Anniversary; Saul Wolfson at 87, an Active Figure in Business, San Antonio Express, June 2, 1918.

Wolfson stayed with the basics. He styled his business as "the only distinctive dry goods house" in San Antonio, but he may have failed to change with the times. His establishment stood in distinct contrast to Joske's. Julius Joske, Wolfson's brother-in-law, had opened a dry goods business a few years after Wolfson, and Wolfson trained both of Joske's sons. One of the Joske sons proved especially able and bought out both his brother and his father. In his hands, Joske's became a full-fledged department store. It acquired its own fleet of delivery vehicles and installed a 3,000-candle searchlight to bring attention to itself.[23] A measure of Joske's relative success was that by the 1920s Wolfson did not own his own building, but rather leased one from Joske's.[24]

And Joske's was not Wolfson's only competitor. Close by was Wolff & Marx. Wolff & Marx introduced an elegant tearoom on its seventh floor, decorated as a Japanese garden. Customers entered by crossing a stone bridge over a rock-lined stream stocked with goldfish. There was also strong competition from Frost Brothers. It sold high-end women's clothes. In 1921, J. C. Penney, the first chain store devoted to clothing and dry goods, opened in San Antonio as well. By this time, J. C. Penney already had more than 300 stores and enjoyed significant economies of scale.[25]

Those who devote their lives to building their own businesses have tried for centuries to pass their firms on to their children, and Wolfson faced a particularly high hurdle. He had married late. He was fifty-four when the first of his four sons was born, and he was already seventy-four before his two oldest sons could join him in the business. By 1923 Saul Wolfson Dry Goods likely had run its course. A creditor began involuntary bankruptcy against it.

By this time, the credit men were accustomed to assessing businesses like Wolfson's. They could turn to Henry Hirshberg, their man who ran the adjustment bureau in San Antonio, to assess matters. Once put into bankruptcy, Wolfson attempted a composition. Compositions

---

[23] See Amy Alves, Joske's Brothers Store: The First Fifty Years, Journal of the Life and Culture of San Antonio, available at www.uiw.edu/sanantonio/JoskesBrothersStore.html.

[24] See https://community.simtropolis.com/forums/topic/69901-dead-and-defeunct-retail-thread/.

[25] Robert J. Gordon, *The Rise and Fall of American Growth: The U.S. Standard of Living Since the Civil War* 90 (Princeton University Press 2016).

could work in the same fashion as the friendly adjustment, but, even though they require consent of the creditors as a group, they could be abused. Hirshberg was on site to object to compositions when the debtor was, in the view of the credit men, unworthy.

Hirshberg was there to object when compositions violated the norms of the credit men even if he could not point to any wrongful act. The credit men put men like him in place to ensure judges refused to confirm a composition if it was not an agreement that creditors as a group, exercising "extreme candor and honesty," would approve if they were attentive.

From Hirshberg's perspective, the composition that Wolfson proposed was suspect. Wolfson offered the business's creditors 40 cents on the dollar in cash for the release of their claims, but the cash needed to pay each creditor this amount ($87,500) was only about $40,000 more than the amount of cash the business had on hand. Moreover, the creditors had already found buyers willing to pay $90,000 for the scheduled assets other than the cash.

There were other reasons to think that Saul Wolfson was not being completely straight. The corporation had been paying Saul Wolfson a salary of $18,000 a year even though he was in his nineties and was no longer active in the day-to-day affairs of the business. In addition, Wolfson had incorporated his business only a year before. This was not itself objectionable, but Wolfson took advantage of the incorporation to enrich himself. He paid Joske's $17,000 a year to lease the store, but he in turn sublet the building to the newly formed corporation for $25,000 a year. In other words, by assigning the lease to the corporation, Wolfson was able to pocket an extra $8,000 a year, the difference between the rent he owed Joske's and the rent his corporation owed him. This amount combined with Wolfson's salary totaled $26,000 a year, not much less than what the creditors were being promised above and beyond the cash the store had on hand.

Such behavior on Wolfson's part suggests why Henry Hirshberg agreed to represent creditors who objected to the composition. As head of the local adjustment bureau, it was not likely that Hirshberg would represent dissident creditors who were arbitrarily refusing to support a sensible composition. The norms of the credit men forbade a creditor from being "uncooperative" in the face of a reasonable proposal from a worthy debtor. Instead, it seems much more likely that Hirshberg was representing creditors who were instead vindicating the norms of the credit men. Wolfson was "dishonest," not in the sense that he lied or engaged in fraud, but because he failed to behave according to their norms. He was unworthy.

Hirshberg successfully argued in the Fifth Circuit that Wolfson's proposed composition was not in the best interests of the creditors, the hurdle that a composition had to clear even after the creditors as a group approved it.[26] The courts' interpretation of the "best interests" language focused on the question of whether the creditors as a group were receiving at least as much under the composition as they would have received if left to their nonbankruptcy remedies. From the credit men's perspective, this did not quite provide them with the oversight that they thought compositions needed and that general principles required.

For the credit men, the failure of Wolfson's plan to give them even as much as they would have received in the event of a liquidation was evidence that the debtor was not doing its utmost to pay what it could. It showed that the creditors who approved it were not themselves being vigilant. That the creditors could have readily received more from a liquidation was a sufficient condition to finding that the plan was not in their best interest, but it was not a necessary one. From the credit men's perspective, irregularities or suspect transactions were alone enough to require further scrutiny and prevent a composition from being approved.[27]

Over time the best interests test weakened further. It became a strictly mechanical test that looked only to what could have been realized if the assets were liquidated. Even then the test was not applied with much rigor. In its modern statutory form, the best interests test gives each dissenting creditor the right to insist on receiving in

---

[26] Fleischmann & Devine, Inc. v. Saul Wolfson Dry Goods Co., Inc., 299 F. 15 (5th Cir. 1924).

[27] See, e.g., Adler v. Jones, 109 F. 967 (6th Cir. 1901); In re Jaffe, 20 F.2d 370 (2d Cir. 1927). Hirshberg was not always successful. In Dilworth v. Boothe, 69 F.2d 621 (5th Cir. 1934), he lost when the appellate court reversed a lower court that had denied a discharge on the ground that the debtor was insufficiently forthright.

a reorganization at least as much as it would have received in a bankruptcy liquidation.[28]

In practice, the protection of the modern best interests test has proved toothless. Every plan of reorganization has pro forma language declaring that it leaves each creditor better off than it would fare in a liquidation, but plan proponents base such assertions on perfunctory expert valuations that posit a liquidation sale that yields little or nothing at all.[29] The credit men wanted to anchor the best interests on a more solid foundation. They wanted judges to do more than ensure an absence of fraud and that everyone had a seat at the table. They wanted judges to assess both the bargain and the circumstances that led up to it. If the debtors were not forthcoming and the creditors as a group were too complacent, when a dissenting creditor raised the alarm, the judge should intervene and put a stop to it.

Saul Wolfson's business did not end well. Wolfson himself died a few months after the bankruptcy began. The composition failed, the business closed its doors, and commerce in San Antonio moved on. Joske's soon ran ads trumpeting its business as the only one in San Antonio for fifty years.

The failure of Saul Wolfson's business did not leave any assets lying idle, however. The business did not own hard assets other than inventory. When the business shut its doors, the building it occupied was soon leased out to someone else. (It became another retail store called "The Fair.")[30] There might be value in the expertise of entrepreneurs like Saul Wolfson's sons, but that expertise does not belong to the creditors, and it remains even if a particular business closes.

If Saul Wolfson's sons wanted to stay in the dry goods business, they needed only to lease another building and persuade a supplier to ship them goods on credit. The value of Wolfson's dry goods business

---

[28] Bankruptcy Code §1129(a)(7). Even though the words "best interests" are no longer in the statute, reorganization lawyers commonly refer to this mandate as the "best interests test." The test does, however, still appear in the chapter governing municipal bankruptcy. See Bankruptcy Code §943(b)(7).

[29] There are some special cases in which the "best interests" test matters because a legal right has a different value in a liquidation.

[30] The Fair itself failed during the Great Depression. It has seen a number of uses over time. The building remains in the heart of San Antonio, not far from the Alamo. It is now the Riverwalk Vista Inn with a large McDonald's and a variety of small retail shops on the ground floor.

over and above what could have been realized in a piecemeal sale of the assets could never have been larger than the cost of forming another corporation, leasing new space, and rehiring the same employees. The costs of recreating the business from scratch put a ceiling on what would be lost if the creditors were able to force a bust-up sale of the business.

The direct legacy of the credit men in shaping the policing power of the judge was modest. Their efforts did not reshape the principles of the Statute of 13 Elizabeth beyond the statutory changes they brought to preference law. The credit men's support of bankruptcy laws, however, gave rise to a new breed of professional. These individuals devoted much of their practice to bankruptcy itself. Over time, lawyers such as Henry Hirshberg came to see themselves as bankruptcy specialists. Just as the credit men were a fraternity committed to a well-functioning credit system, these lawyers saw themselves as committed to an effective bankruptcy system.[31]

These new professionals came to believe that bankruptcy was not merely a backstop for the friendly adjustment. If properly crafted, bankruptcy law, like the equity receivership, could provide a forum in which they could sort out the problems of a distressed debtor. The law as it existed at the time of Saul Wolfson's failure fell short of this goal, but these professionals came to believe that sensible bankruptcy reform could bring it about. In the next chapter, the focus turns to how a handful of these individuals, along with those who represented investment bankers and two particularly energetic New Deal lawyers, brought about the next wave of bankruptcy reform.

---

[31] Hirshberg himself ultimately became a bankruptcy referee, the precursor to the modern bankruptcy judge.

4 A NEW DEAL

The investment bankers who provided capital for the great railroads and the credit men who managed many billions of dollars of trade debt each year both loomed large in the United States' economic life in the first decades of the twentieth century. Both saw formal legal processes as decidedly second best. Investment bankers and the credit men preferred to work things out consensually. In the case of investment bankers, this took the form of an exchange offer. Investors would be persuaded to give up their existing securities for new ones that possessed the same value, but which were more in line with the cash flows of the firm. In the case of the credit men, there were friendly adjustments. The local credit bureau would reach a deal with worthy debtors and local creditors. They would be paid what was possible, and worthy debtors could continue in business.

The investment bankers and the credit men both believed the sensible path was to work collectively to sort out the problems of a distressed debtor. Notwithstanding this much common ground, however, they had dramatically different views about the kind of backstop that the law should provide. These took them on different paths of law reform.

The investment bankers did not need or want judges to exercise greater oversight of their reorganizations. From their perspective, the intrusions that the Supreme Court required in cases like *Boyd* – such as giving voice to out-of-the-money creditors who were not part of the firm going forward – were unwelcome. But the investment bankers and their professionals accepted the core idea that negotiations between the debtor and its creditors should not run afoul of the principles embedded in the Statute of 13 Elizabeth. Moreover, they could live with the somewhat more demanding interpretation of the Statute that the Supreme Court imposed. Their concern was with the absence of a secure statutory foundation on which these unwritten principles rested.

The equity receivership worked only because judges were willing to look the other way in the face of a number of technical legal infirmities. Judges might not do this forever. Moreover, the fiction of the foreclosure sale required that actual cash be raised when some senior creditors refused to join the senior committee. This made no sense when the foreclosure sale was merely a hollow ritual.

For their part, the credit men found that the bankruptcy law that they needed to deter local creditors from grabbing assets at their expense had not worked as they had hoped. The credit men pushed for a number of incremental reforms. They wanted amendments that further deterred fraudulent behavior on the part of the debtor and further limited the ability of creditors to jump the gun.

These two sets of players, however, were not the only ones who were to concern themselves with law reform. Academics who came to Washington as part of the New Deal ultimately joined their efforts to effect change in the bankruptcy law, and they came with a radically different agenda. They believed a firmer regulatory hand was needed, especially in large cases. They saw the law's chief mission as one of protecting the unsophisticated investors who held securities in distressed companies. *Boyd* had given all investors a chance to participate in the bargaining, but distant individuals saving for their retirement were too far away from the action and too unfamiliar with the mysteries of corporate reorganization for this theoretical right to do them much good. Someone needed to be on site to champion their interests. The interplay between these New Deal reformers and these other two contending groups dramatically reshaped reorganization law during the 1930s.[1] It is useful to examine each in turn, starting with the professionals who shepherded large firms through equity receiverships.

[1] David Skeel's masterful history of bankruptcy law provides an account of the developments set out in this chapter from a different perspective. See David A. Skeel, Jr., *Debt's Dominion* 73–100 (Princeton University Press 2001).

The lawyers for the investment bankers had long feared the entire structure of the equity receivership might collapse if judges were to poke too hard. By the late 1920s, they were becoming increasingly uneasy. In the first instance, they feared that courts might strike down the use of equity receiverships to restructure distressed businesses altogether. Of particular concern was the opinion Justice Benjamin Cardozo issued in *Shapiro v. Wilgus*.[2] The case involved an individual debtor who was financially distressed and who sought relief by transferring the assets of his business to a newly formed corporation and then putting the corporation through an equity receivership. Justice Cardozo held the series of transfers was a fraudulent conveyance. From his perspective, the transaction was no different from what Blair McClenachan tried to do in *Burd v. Smith*. In both cases, an individual debtor is turning assets over to a receiver in order to buy time. But Justice Cardozo did not distinguish the case before him from the typical equity receivership. In every receivership, a distressed debtor turns its assets over to a receiver to buy time. A statute that explicitly authorized equity receiverships would make sure that *Shapiro v. Wilgus* could not be extended to prevent them.

A statute could also allay other concerns of the Wall Street lawyers. For example, it was not even clear that a federal court even had jurisdiction over the typical equity receivership. The only plausible font of federal jurisdiction was diversity jurisdiction. A federal court had the power to oversee an equity receivership only because the litigants were citizens of different states. The lawyers had successfully argued that diversity existed when the railroad was incorporated in one state and the general creditor who began the receivership was a citizen of another. But one could argue that diversity existed only if all the creditors of the railroad were citizens of a state other than that of the railroad. As long as some creditors were citizens of the same state as the railroad, as was virtually always the case, diversity might not exist.

There were other reasons to doubt that the equity receivership rested on solid legal foundations. The equity receivership mechanism worked only as long as judges were willing to accept all of the various fictions it employed. Judges had to accept that there was a genuine

---

[2] Shapiro v. Wilgus, 287 U.S. 348 (1932). See also Harkin v. Brundage, 276 U.S. 36 (1928).

dispute between the petitioning creditor and the corporation, even though this creditor was acting only at the behest of the corporation itself. And, of course, the judge also had to accept the idea that the receiver was conducting a sale, even though everyone understood that the only bidder would be the committee of senior bondholders, and they would credit-bid rather than put up cash. Finally, the judge had to be untroubled that the firm was not in fact going to end up with the senior creditors (those who were the high bidders at the "sale") and instead was going to be distributed according to a scheme that included the old shareholders.

In addition to worrying about the equity receivership's somewhat shaky premises, the Wall Street lawyers who did corporate reorganizations – in particular Paul Cravath and Robert Swaine, the two lawyers who suc-ceeded Victor Morawetz at his firm, hoped that embedding a reorganization regime in a statute would allow the appointment of a single receiver in each case. In the absence of a statute, a railroad that spanned multiple jurisdictions had to have multiple receivers. Having a single receiver would save time and money.

Cravath and Swaine also believed that a statute could increase the efficiency of receiverships in one additional way. Under the existing regime, cash was required for every senior claim that had not been turned over to the protective committee and therefore could not be folded into the credit bid. This was not always easy even when the upset price was low relative to the value of the firm. Cravath and Swaine thought it would be far preferable if the dissenters could be forced to take shares in the reorganized entity instead of cash. This would be possible only if a statute allowed the sale mechanism to be bypassed.[3]

Congress passed §77 for railroads and §77B for other types of corporations. These gave Cravath and Swaine and other restructuring professionals most of what they wanted.[4] Instead of a foreclosure sale in which the senior committee bought the assets of the business at an artificially low price, holders of each class of claims would vote on the plan that emerged from the negotiations among the members of the

---

[3] See Robert T. Swaine, Corporate Reorganization Under the Federal Bankruptcy Power, 19 Va. L. Rev. 317, 327–28 (1933).

[4] Act of March 3, 1933, ch. 204, §77, 47 Stat. 1467, 1474; Act of June 7, 1934, ch. 424, §77B, 48 Stat. 911, 912.

various protective committees. The plan would set out the ownership structure the firm would have after the reorganization. If enough creditors voted in favor of the plan, the judge would then assess the plan and determine whether it was "fair and equitable," did not "discriminate unfairly in favor of any class of creditors or stockholders," and was "feasible." If it satisfied those requirements, the plan could be confirmed without the ritual of a foreclosure sale.

The requirement that the plan be "fair and equitable" echoes the language judges had used in cases such as *Paton* when they approved equity receiverships. Courts would retain the same power to ensure that the plan was not devised by a debtor and one creditor with the aim of undermining the rights of others. It would also, consistent with *Boyd*, require the judge to ensure that everyone had a seat at the table.

At the same time Cravath and Swaine pushed for these reforms, the credit men expanded their adjustment bureaus and continued to rely on "friendly adjustments." They also worked for incremental bankruptcy reform and succeeded in bringing about some changes to the 1898 Act. Bankruptcy law had always denied discharges to debtors who lied to their creditors. The credit men persuaded Congress to make fraud on credit-reporting agencies an additional ground for denying individual debtors the right to discharge their debts.

Such reforms were in the first instance focused not on the ability of the bankruptcy process to help creditors recover what they were owed, but rather on making fraud less likely in the first place. The credit men believed such laws would make debtors (and the local creditors and local banks they tended to favor over the credit men) more likely to cooperate with them.

The lawyers who worked for the credit men recognized that the bankruptcy process itself, even if well-conceived in theory, was not working well in practice. Costs were high, and recoveries were often embarrassingly modest. Moreover, in some places, lawyers who appeared in bankruptcy court were too often not honorable representatives of the credit men like Henry Hirshberg, but rather members of a "bankruptcy ring" who enriched themselves at the expense of creditors.

Especially in large cities like New York, the defects in bankruptcy practice were hard to ignore. When a business failed and filed for bankruptcy, the federal district judge had to appoint a receiver. The power to appoint receivers in bankruptcy cases was an opportunity for patronage. Judges were tempted to appoint friends or friends of the politicians who put them on the bench. And even the best-intentioned judges might not have the skill needed to find able receivers. The job required marketing as well as legal skill, and judges had no expertise with respect to discerning the former.

Most creditors were owed relatively little and did not become involved in the case. Their expected returns were too low to justify the time it took to take stock of the debtor's affairs. And even if a creditor did spend the time and take part in the bankruptcy process, in cities like New York they would find the same small group of lawyers working in concert against them. The "bankruptcy ring" might not hold a large portion of the debt, but there would be enough of them to outvote anyone else who bothered to appear.

This world was cozy and corrupt.[5] The members of the ring controlled the vote over such matters as who would serve as trustee, and they voted for a trustee who would in turn hire lawyers who belonged to the ring. When the credit men appeared in sufficient number, the members of the bankruptcy ring would move for a delay of the meeting and force them to appear again and again until they gave up. The assets of the debtor were eventually sold at an auction, but the auction did not yield much. Again, the members of the ring would appear at the auction and bid collusively.

Distributions to creditors were small, and the administrative expenses were high. *Goody Stores* was a typical case of the era. Goody Stores was a chain of candy stores and restaurants with debts of $300,000. The district judge, Francis A. Winslow, appointed E. Bright Wilson as receiver, as he had in many other cases. Wilson hired three lawyers, including, as had been his practice, one who had also been appointed by Judge Winslow as a receiver in many other cases and who had similarly hired Wilson as his lawyer in those.[6] He also

---

[5] For example, Judge Grover M. Moscowitz gave eighteen of his twenty biggest receiverships to his former law partner. See Strongin on Stand in Moscowitz Case, New York Times, June 19, 1929, at 33.

[6] Thomas Clifford Billig, What Price Bankruptcy: A Plea for "Friendly Adjustment," 14 *Cornell L. Rev.* 413, 422 (1929).

hired Stuart Eaton as an appraiser. Eaton had no experience as an appraiser, but he was Judge Winslow's stepson. Wilson paid little attention to the case, and his recordkeeping was casual. Eaton ended up with a Packard automobile. Three years after the bankruptcy filing, there still had not been any distributions to the creditors.

When all of this became public, Judge Winslow resigned under threat of impeachment. His son-in-law was disbarred, as was Wilson. More important, these scandals led to an investigation of the bankruptcy ring in New York. Heading it was Judge Thomas Thacher. He was the son of the founder of the Wall Street firm of Simpson Thacher, and he was later to serve as solicitor general under President Herbert Hoover.

Thacher appointed William J. Donovan to spearhead the investigation. Donovan had won the Congressional Medal of Honor in the Great War and later went on to found the Office of Strategic Services, the precursor of the CIA. Donovan in turn brought on two young associates, George S. Leisure, who later became a partner of Donovan at the firm he founded that year (the storied white-shoe law firm Donovan Leisure), and Lloyd K. Garrison. Garrison went on to become dean of the Wisconsin Law School and the first head of the National Labor Relations Board. He later practiced at Paul Weiss (the full name of which remains Paul, Weiss, Rifkind, Wharton, and Garrison). These investigators were a group of high-powered, reform-minded lawyers, but they had little bankruptcy expertise.

The investigations produced a report in 1930. When Judge Thacher became solicitor general, he made Garrison a special assistant attorney general to continue the inquiry. This led to another report, in December 1931 (commonly called the Thacher or Thacher-Garrison report). It recommended comprehensive bankruptcy reform. President Hoover embraced the report, and the bill that it proposed was introduced into the House and Senate in 1932.[7]

There were many honorable bankruptcy professionals and able bankruptcy referees who had no patience for the bankruptcy rings, but the Thacher-Garrison report proposed creating an agency within

---

[7] This was the Hastings-Michener Bill. See Henry J. Friendly, Some Comments on the Corporate Reorganizations Act, 48 *Harv. L. Rev.* 39, 49–50 (1943).

the executive branch to oversee the administration of bankruptcy cases. This would upend bankruptcy practice, an unsettling feature from the perspective of existing bankruptcy referees. As eager as the best of them were to be rid of bankruptcy rings, they had little enthusiasm for law reform that would put them out of work. An administrative agency based in Washington would do this.

The Thacher-Garrison report hit an especially raw nerve with Paul King, one of the two bankruptcy referees in Detroit. King set out to build opposition to it. King pointed out to supporters of the reform proposal that the particular problem that had sparked outrage in New York – the way that the power to appoint receivers led to patronage, with its attendant incompetence and, in some cases, corruption – was one the court in Detroit had solved by appointing a single institutional receiver. By appointing a single institution to be a receiver in all cases, the court disabled itself from granting patronage in any particular case.[8] And the federal court in New York followed this example even before Donovan began his investigation.

King argued that running the bankruptcy system out of Washington would not remove patronage from the administration of bankruptcy, but rather centralize it. As King characterized it: "If this thing goes through as it is, the organization could be made into the niftiest little political machine that ever was put together, with the ten lieutenants in the persons of the proposed ten administrators, and the 200 or 400 or 600 examiners as captains, and the small army of authorized trustees in every part of the country."[9]

King wrote a digest of the proposed amendments, which he printed at his own expense. He entered into an extensive correspondence with those whose work brought them within the orbit of the bankruptcy system,[10] and he did everything else he could to keep it from being enacted.

---

[8] Bank to Be Receiver in All Failures Here, New York Times, January 17, 1929, pp. 1, 10; Thomas Clifford Billig, supra note 6, at 417–18 (1929).

[9] Letter from Paul King to Burt D. Dady, May 12, 1932, quoted in John D. Honsberger, The Origins of the National Bankruptcy Conference: A Hinge-Point of Change 1932–1933, unpublished (1985), p. 10.

[10] They included Robert A. B. Cook of Boston, who was the chair of the Bankruptcy Committee of the Commercial Law League, and Jacob M. Lashly, the chair of the Committee on Commercial Law and Bankruptcy of the American Bar Association.

King's hard work led to the defeat of the reforms of the Thacher-Garrison report. The only bankruptcy reforms that Congress passed were §77 and §77B, the provisions governing railroads and other large reorganizations. As noted, these provided a statutory foundation for existing equity receivership practice, something that mattered to Cravath and Swaine but was of little interest to men like King. Garrison left government to become dean of the law school at the University of Wisconsin. Thacher returned to private practice at the end of the Hoover administration. Franklin Roosevelt came to Washington, and his administration had no interest in reintroducing any legislation with Hoover's fingerprints on it. Thanks to King's efforts, bankruptcy reform appeared dead.

It might seem that, once free from the threat posed by reform-minded lawyers, Paul King's job was done. He could return to Detroit and continue his life as a bankruptcy referee. But this misunderstands what Paul King was about. To be sure, King's vision of a sensible bankruptcy law was one that preserved bankruptcy referees and hence his own job. The contrary vision of the Thacher-Garrison report made it unacceptable. Nevertheless, Paul King genuinely believed in bankruptcy reform. He continued to promote bankruptcy reform long after the Thacher-Garrison proposals were defeated.

Like many of his contemporaries, Paul King did not bowl alone.[11] Paul King was a joiner. He was a Freemason, a Knight Templar, and a Shriner. He was president of the Detroit Council of Churches. He was a Rotarian (and served as director and president of the Rotary Club in Detroit). He organized and conducted the First World Congress for Workers for Crippled Children in Geneva in 1929, the second in The Hague in 1931, and a third in Budapest in 1936.

Paul King was someone naturally drawn to worthy causes, and one of them was bankruptcy reform. King had already organized the bankruptcy judges by creating the National Association of Referees in Bankruptcy. Its journal remains the leading journal devoted to bankruptcy law. Its annual conference continues to bring more than a thousand reorganization professionals together each year. In addition

---

[11] For a discussion of the decline of fraternal and other organizations that bind communities together, see Robert D. Putnam, *Bowling Alone: The Collapse and Revival of American Community* (Simon and Schuster 2000).

to organizing referees, King served as chair of the committee on bankruptcy and on the section on commercial law of the American Bar Association, as well as many other bar groups.

The defeat of the Thacher-Garrison bill did nothing to extinguish King's enthusiasm for bankruptcy reform. King reached out to other bankruptcy professionals. He found kindred spirits among fellow lawyers and judges who wanted to improve the system and who, like him, were willing to devote considerable time and energy to the enterprise. King also enlisted the credit men. Of course, the credit men for the most part wanted to avoid bankruptcy. They much preferred "friendly adjustments." Nevertheless, they wanted to strengthen the backstop that bankruptcy law provided and offered King some support. Among other things, the credit men wanted to broaden preference law and make it harder for creditors to take secret liens to gain an advantage for themselves.

Members of Congress who came to Washington in the wake of Roosevelt's election welcomed King's efforts. Bankruptcy reform was something worth thinking about in the midst of the Great Depression. Congressmen themselves lacked the expertise to know what reforms made sense, and they were willing to defer to those the law was intended to help. But before they could defer to them, these intended beneficiaries needed to reach a consensus about the shape reform should take.

The chair of the joint committee urged Paul King and other likeminded lawyers to join forces and return with draft legislation. King formed another fraternal organization, the National Bankruptcy Conference. Its founding members included representatives of the Commercial Law League, the Referees Association, the credit men, the bankruptcy section of the ABA, and a law professor (Harvard's James McLaughlin).

The dynamics of law reform have changed substantially in the decades since Paul King held sway, and fraternal groups that he was quick to join have fallen out of favor. The National Bankruptcy Conference, however, lives on.[12] Its members still assemble at least once a year. It remains small, never having more than seventy

---

[12] I was invited to become a member of the NBC in 1993 and was elected its chair in 2020.

members. To be sure, it no longer wields the influence it once had. It and other reform groups were ignored when Congress radically changed consumer bankruptcy law in 2005. But the National Bankruptcy Conference still has the ear of Congress. Along with other groups, such as the American Bankruptcy Institute, it persuaded Congress to pass a major overhaul of the provisions governing small business reorganizations in 2019.

Paul King ensured that the National Bankruptcy Conference, like any other fraternity, establish its own rituals, and it did. New members, for example, must entertain everyone with a speech about how they will improve the organization when they attend their first annual dinner. The presentations typically take a humorous turn. A newly admitted law professor gives a mock academic lecture. Another new conferee appears dressed as a well-known politician and gives a talk making fun of this politician's views of bankruptcy. Such bonding rituals ensured that all "check their clients at the door."

Members of the National Bankruptcy Conference embraced incremental reforms. They wanted in the first instance bankruptcy law to discourage last-minute grabs that undermined "friendly adjustments." Reforms in preference law could make it easier to claw back payments to creditors who were either close to the debtor or who engaged in self-help while everyone else was working together. Useful statutory reforms might also include putting into the statute sensible practices, such as providing for the formation of committees that could bring different types of creditors together and allow each group to speak with a single voice. Additional mechanisms might be added to ensure that the debtor was not able to dissipate assets while the bargaining between the creditors and the owner-manager was ongoing.

Compositions like the one used for Saul Wolfson might prove useful if the judge were able to guard against abuse. They could provide a sensible way to keep a worthy debtor in business even when some of the creditors refused to cooperate. If creditors as a group could reach a deal with an entrepreneur, everyone could be better off, even if there were a few dissenters. Instead of liquidating the business, the creditors would accept cash or notes that would leave them better off and allow the owner-manager to go on as before.

Paul King warmed to the challenge of reaching a consensus among a group of like-minded individuals and then bringing it back to Congress. All of this took time, however, and while he was engaged in these efforts, a third voice of reform could be heard. It came from among the young lawyers who came to Washington during the New Deal.[13]

Among the New Deal reformers, there were two whose particular expertise lay in corporate reorganizations: Jerome Frank and William O. Douglas. Jerome Frank was born in 1889. He went to the University of Chicago Law School and, while there, also worked as a secretary to a Chicago alderman. "Against the likes of aldermen popularly known as Hinky Dink and Bath House John, Frank honed a political style that was never to be known for its subtlety nor its reticence."[14]

After graduation, Frank entered private practice in Chicago, where he focused on corporate reorganizations. He restructured not only large railroads, but also industrial firms that were financed with publicly traded securities. Public investors held the debt of these firms, while the insiders who controlled the firm held the equity. This experience left Frank with a decidedly skeptical view of reorganization law.

Frank moved to New York, where he underwent psychoanalysis and wrote *Law and the Modern Mind*, one of the classics of legal realism. At the same time, he worked as a research associate at the Yale Law School. At Yale, Frank met William O. Douglas, who taught corporate reorganizations there. They were kindred spirits. Douglas had worked for Robert Swaine before coming to Yale, and he shared Frank's dark view of restructuring practice. They soon joined many lawyers who moved to Washington to help the Roosevelt administration craft the New Deal.

Douglas started at the Securities and Exchange Commission and eventually persuaded Frank to join him there. At the SEC, they produced a seven-volume report cataloguing abuses in equity receiverships. Their overriding concern was to find a way to protect small

---

[13] An excellent account of these New Deal reformers can be found in David A. Skeel, Jr., *Debt's Dominion* 101–26 (Princeton University Press 2001).

[14] Joel Seligman, *The Transformation of Wall Street: A History of the Securities and Exchange Commission and Modern Corporate Finance* 215 (Houghton Mifflin 1982).

investors when a firm attempted to restructure their bonds in a receivership.

Small investors did not figure large in the great railroad receiverships. Before the Great War, those who provided capital to large enterprises were large institutional investors like insurance companies or banks. Many were located in England or Europe. After the Great War, however, the United States was no longer a debtor nation. Capital no longer flowed from Europe to the United States. Increasingly the investors were individuals trying to build a nest egg.

These investors suffered massive losses during the Great Depression. The New Deal reformers believed that these individuals needed protecting. Their view was in keeping with the thinking of other liberal reformers. There were a number of popular books that recounted the failures of large firms and the huge costs of restructuring them. These included Max Lowenthal's *The Investor Pays*, which harshly criticized the receivership of the Chicago, Milwaukee, and St. Paul Railway Co.,[15] as well as Thurman Arnold's *Folklore of Capitalism*.

Robert Swaine and his fellow Wall Street lawyers believed they brought value both when they raised capital for firms and when they helped restructure them. Most of their ventures were successful, and when a venture failed, they were there to sort out the mess. Their knowledge of the firm and its finances meant that they were the ones best equipped to represent the firm in bad times as well as in good ones.

But the New Deal reformers saw things differently. For them, the world of investment bankers and their professionals was entirely too cozy. Earning fees from issuing and restructuring the same bonds was, from their point of view, double dipping. A neutral expert was better positioned to put things right and protect the unsophisticated.

During this era, the market for securities was largely unregulated. The reformers believed that gullible members of the public were all too often tricked into putting their money into dubious business ventures. Regulation of the securities markets was needed to ensure that public investors were adequately informed before parting with their savings. At the same time, small investors needed protection when firms were

---

[15] Max Lowenthal, *The Investor Pays* (Alfred A. Knopf 1933).

reorganized. Without such protection, investment bankers, their law-yers, and corporate insiders would, the reformers believed, continue to take advantage of small investors. As Thurman Arnold described it:

> The fees represent high-class boondoggling and bureaucratic red tape of so complicated a nature that it is almost impossible to say at what point they are unjustified. . . . The stakes of participation in reorganization have become so high that they often are a greater objective than the reorganization itself. The situation is very similar to the control of a municipal government by a political machine, with the possible exception that public opinion does not permit politicians to take any such percentage of the income of the muni-cipality which they control.[16]

Frank and Douglas believed the sensible path to reducing the costs of reorganizing firms was to ban investment bankers and their profes-sionals from returning to a business for which they had raised the capital when the time came to restructure it. They also wanted to institute tighter judicial and regulatory supervision as a general matter. The judge's power to oversee restructuring negotiations had to be expanded dramatically.

Merely ensuring that everyone had a chance to participate and enforce whatever bargain emerged was not enough. The reformers believed that the judge should examine every aspect of the reorganiza-tion bargain and intervene to protect outside investors. As Frank explained in an article that he wrote attacking Robert Swaine:

> There is every reason why that court should approve and foster active supervision by the lower courts of reorganizations so as to protect the average security holder who is otherwise helpless. Courts of equity have a tradition of aiding the helpless, such as infants, idiots and drunkards. The average security holder in a corporate reorganization is of like kind.[17]

Frank and Douglas put the Wall Street lawyers on the defensive. Douglas boasted that after one hearing, Robert Swaine complained that he had been held upside-down and had been shaken until his

---

[16] Thurman W. Arnold, *The Folklore of Capitalism* 258–59 (Yale University Press 1937).
[17] Jerome N. Frank, Some Realistic Reflections on Some Aspects of Corporate Reorganization, 19 *Va. L. Rev.* 541, 569 (1933).

fillings fell out.[18] Politically savvy, Frank and Douglas made common cause with Paul King and the National Bankruptcy Conference. The New Dealers had little interest in the problems of the credit men and their small business debtors. These were not firms in which small investors invested their savings. For their part, Paul King and his fraternal brothers were not involved with large reorganizations. The businesses of interest to them had mostly trade debt. Investment bankers were altogether absent. The shareholders were individual entrepreneurs. When New Deal reformers and the National Bankruptcy Conference spoke with a single voice, however, they could command the attention of Congress. It was a marriage of convenience. Both groups wanted bankruptcy reform, and although the reforms each group wanted did not overlap, they did not conflict either. With their support, Congress put in place massive bankruptcy reforms in 1938 with the passage of the Chandler Act.

Many of the small business reforms were implemented with specific changes to the text of the bankruptcy law. These were largely aimed at deterring misbehavior by debtors and gun-jumping by local creditors. In addition, Paul King pushed to expand the ability of businesses to restructure once in bankruptcy. These became Chapter XI.[19] It replaced the composition provision at work in Saul Wolfson's bankruptcy. The typical Chapter XI case was again a small business whose identity was tied to the entrepreneur who ran and owned it.[20] Chapter XI made possible the reorganization of small businesses in the same fashion as a friendly adjustment. It could be useful when opposition to a restructuring came not from the credit men as a group, but rather from a few dissident creditors intent upon throwing sand in the gears.

Douglas and Frank had little interest in the reorganization of these small business bankruptcies. These businesses had no public investors, small or otherwise, and they were happy to acquiesce in the reforms that King and others advanced. Douglas and Frank focused on large

---

[18] William O. Douglas, *Go East, Young Man* 260 (Random House 1974).

[19] By convention, the chapters of the 1898 Act are denoted with Roman numerals, while those of the 1978 Bankruptcy Code are referred to by Hindu-Arabic numerals. As discussed in Chapter 7 of this book, modern Chapter 11 emerged from both Chapters X and XI.

[20] The bankruptcy judge had the ability to appoint a receiver to take over the operations of the firm, but the normal practice that emerged was to allow the debtor to remain in place.

firms. Their reforms led to Chapter X. Chapter X included a strong oversight role for the SEC and required the appointment of an independent trustee to run each firm while it was being reorganized.

For Douglas and Frank, however, statutory reform was only part of the story. Also central to their conception of the reorganization of large firms was strong judicial oversight. They believed that the principles of the Statute of 13 Elizabeth required more than the Supreme Court had demanded in *Howard, Monon,* and *Boyd.* Judges overseeing the reorganization of large businesses should ensure that everyone's interests were protected, especially those of small public investors. It was not enough just to offer everyone a seat at the table. Even if they had the time and the resources needed to participate, small investors would be too easily outmatched by Wall Street professionals who possessed both expertise and inside knowledge. Judges had to take a more active part in each case. They needed to police the bargaining aggressively to make sure that the rights of outside investors were protected.

The legislation Congress enacted did not explicitly give judges these expanded powers, but Douglas and Frank thought judges already possessed them. For them, these powers followed from a proper understanding of first principles. Douglas was appointed to the Supreme Court soon after the passage of the Chandler Act. From this position, he needed only to persuade four of his brethren on the Supreme Court that judges possessed these powers to make his conception of them a reality.

As a Justice of the Supreme Court, Douglas expanded the reach of the judge's oversight power. This power was still anchored in the Statute of 13 Elizabeth,[21] but it was much more sweeping. As Douglas explained in one case: "A bankruptcy court is a court of equity and is guided by equitable doctrines and principles. ... A court of equity may in its discretion in the exercise of the jurisdiction committed to it grant or deny relief upon performance of a condition which will safeguard the public interest."[22] Even though that case dealt with

---

[21] Douglas specifically invokes the Statute of 13 Elizabeth in Pepper v. Litton, 308 U.S. 295 (1939) ("The findings of the District Court, amply supported by the evidence, reveal a scheme to defraud creditors reminiscent of some of the evils with which 13 Eliz. c.5 was designed to cope").

[22] Securities and Exchange Commission v. United States Realty & Improvement Co., 310 U.S. 434, 455 (1940).

prepetition misconduct, Douglas used the case as an occasion to underscore the broad powers of the bankruptcy court to exercise control over all aspects of the case.

As Douglas explained in *Pepper v. Litton*, these powers had to be "invoked to the end that fraud will not prevail, that substance will not give way to form, that technical considerations will not prevent substantial justice from being done." Hence, "[i]n the exercise of its equitable jurisdiction the bankruptcy court has the power to sift the circumstances surrounding any claim to see that injustice or unfairness is not done in administration of the bankrupt estate."[23]

In Douglas's view, the judge was required to scrutinize "the circumstances surrounding the acceptances, the special or ulterior motives which may have induced them, the time of acquiring the claims so voting, and the amount paid therefor, and the like." He elaborated:

> Where such investigation discloses the existence of unfair dealing, a breach of fiduciary obligations, profiting from a trust, special benefits for the reorganizers, or the need for protection of investors against an inside few or of one class of investors from the encroachments of another, the court has ample power to adjust the remedy to meet the need. ... It is not dependent on express statutory provisions. It inheres in the jurisdiction of a court of bankruptcy. The necessity for its exercise is based on the responsibility of the court ... to be satisfied that the plan in its practical incidence embodies a fair and equitable bargain openly arrived at and devoid of overreaching, however subtle.[24]

Douglas believed that these inherent powers gave the court the power to disallow or subordinate the claim of a creditor who thwarted the rights of others. A court had to use its powers to ensure that those who engaged in bargaining did not engage in advantage-taking. Moreover, and of continuing relevance today, the judge must ensure that the parties focus on the debtor while they are negotiating. They cannot pursue other agendas while they sit at the bargaining table, whether otherwise benign or not.

---

[23] 308 U.S. at 305, 307–08.
[24] American United Mutual Life Insurance Co. v. City of Avon Park, 311 U.S. 138, 146 (1940).

Texas Hotel Securities Corp. v. Waco Development illustrates one sort
of behavior that was out of bounds.[25] *Waco* revolved around a fight
over the Roosevelt Hotel in Waco, Texas. In the late 1920s, Conrad
Hilton was beginning his career as a hotelier. He had already taken over
several run-down hotels in Texas and successfully renovated them.
A group of local businessmen in Waco acquired an old hotel and
brought Hilton in to work his magic. Hilton bought the hotel from
them, built a new tower, and added air-conditioning to public spaces.
The renovated hotel opened in 1927.[26]

The Great Depression hit the hotel business hard, however. Hilton
had to sell the hotel property back to the businessmen. He retained
a ninety-nine-year lease and remained responsible for paying off the
mortgage. As bad economic times continued, business continued to
decline. Under Hilton's management the hotel did make enough to
meet the mortgage payments, but revenues were insufficient to make
the lease payments. The Waco businessmen went to state court and
were able to oust Hilton for his failure to pay the rent. But the local
businessmen soon found themselves in an even worse position than
Hilton. They could not even make the mortgage payments. They
attempted to restructure the debtor under §77B, the reorganization
regime that bridged the time between the equity receivership and the
Chandler Act.

Hilton tried to regain control of the hotel while it was in §77B
reorganization. He bought a blocking position in one of the impaired
classes and voted against the plan, pressing instead for one that would
return him to the management of the hotel. The Texas businessmen
objected and argued that Hilton should not be able to cast his vote as he
had. An appellate court rejected their argument.

Douglas was still at the SEC at the time of this reorganization, but
the observations he made to Congress about the case illustrate the
conception of the judge's role that he brought to the Supreme Court.

---

[25] 87 F.2d 395 (5th Cir. 1936).
[26] Geoff Hunt, Texas Over Time: "The Roosevelt Tower, Waco, TX," Baylor University
Texas Collection blog, March 6, 2018, https://blogs.baylor.edu/texascollection/2018/03/
06/texas-over-time-the-roosevelt-tower-waco-tx/; Amanda Sawyer, Roosevelt Hotel,
Baylor University Waco History blog, accessed August 12, 2021, https://wacohistory
.org/items/show/41.

Douglas found Hilton's behavior objectionable, and he faulted the court for failing to put a stop to it.[27] In Douglas's view, investors must cast their votes and otherwise conduct themselves in a fashion that advanced only their interests as investors. They had to cabin off their other interests. They must focus on their stake in the business. They cannot pursue some other agenda.

Variations on the facts of *Waco* make plain the concern that animated Douglas. Imagine that, instead of wanting to manage the hotel, Hilton owned a competing hotel next to Roosevelt Hotel. He buys a blocking position in one class of bonds in order to ensure that the Roosevelt Hotel could never reorganize successfully. Under these facts, when Hilton votes against a plan, he is advancing his own economic interests in a competitor, not his interests as a stakeholder in the Roosevelt. Indeed, he is willing to sacrifice that interest. Douglas believed that acting in such a fashion was out of bounds. Those who vote in a reorganization have to put on blinders with respect to their outside interests.

Taking such a view of how investors must act goes beyond what the Supreme Court required in *Boyd*. *Boyd* just ensured that everyone had a right to participate in the bargaining. Under Douglas's view, the judge must do more. The judge must review the behavior of each of the parties at the bargaining table and ensure they are advancing only their stake in the business and not some other goal that exists apart from it. Douglas believed that Hilton's rights as a holder of debt of the hotel and his interest in managing the hotel were two different things. Hence, Hilton should not have been able to cast his votes in the former capacity to advance his interests in the latter.

Douglas's approach, one he brought with him to the Supreme Court, relies critically on the ability of the judge to identify when parties are not acting in a way that advances their interests as stakeholders in the business. It is clear enough when a competitor participates in

---

[27] Testimony of SEC Commissioner Douglas, Revision of the Bankruptcy Act: Hearing on H.R. 6439 Before the House Comm. on the Judiciary, 75th Cong. 181–82 (1937) (Courts should have the ability "to affirm a plan over the opposition of a minority attempting to block the adoption of a plan merely for selfish purposes. The *Waco* case ... was such a situation").

a reorganization to destroy a rival, but rarely are the facts so clear, as *Waco* itself illustrates.

Douglas failed to see that Hilton might have voted as he did because he believed that his management skills brought value. Hilton might well have believed that the Roosevelt might be worth more if he ran it than if the Waco businessmen did. Hilton's insistence upon being brought back to manage the hotel might be entirely consistent with maximizing the value of his stake in the business. Indeed, Hilton's subsequent success in moving beyond Texas and establishing a worldwide hotel empire is strong evidence to this effect. Facts are never as easy for a judge to grasp as Douglas thought.

Douglas's view of the judge's inherent power to prevent an ulterior motive from intruding into the bargaining space prevailed. Contemporary judges remain attentive to the possibility that an investor is doing more than protecting the value of the investment it has in a business. They are especially alert when a buyer enters who wants to use the reorganization process to gain control of the entire business.

The following example illustrates the type of mischief that the judge should prevent. A company faces hard times. It has defaulted on debt payments and needs fixing. If put under competent management, it is worth $360. This would be enough to pay each of the creditors in full. All the creditors know the company is worth $360, and so does an outsider who wants to buy the business. But the value of the firm is not known to the world at large and not to the judge. No other buyer is going to pay even as much as $240 for this property. The various creditors are scattered and cannot make common cause with each other.

The one outsider who has knowledge of the business's true value persuades the old equityholder, the person in control of the debtor, to support a plan in which the assets of the business are to be sold to it for $240. Persuasion can take many forms. The outsider might, for example, offer to retain the old equityholder as a consultant if it succeeds in buying the firm. The outsider makes it clear that the burdens will not be especially time-consuming. It promises to call only if the day ever comes when it believes that the old equityholder, who ran the company into the ground, can provide useful advice.

None of the existing creditors is happy about the sale to the outsider. Each can vote against this plan, and if they all were committed to one another to take this course, they could keep the outsider from being successful and instead put in place a plan in which each would ultimately be paid in full. The business is in fact worth $360, and each knows it.

But the creditors have no way to make common cause with one another, and the outsider can exploit this with a divide-and-conquer strategy. The outsider can tell each and every one of the creditors:

> What matters is not your vote, but what all the others do. If they vote against the plan to sell the business to me, you will end up being paid 100 cents on the dollar. But if they vote in favor of the sale to me, you're only going to get 67 cents on the dollar. (I'll buy the firm for $240. That cash will be distributed pro rata to you. Because the creditors as a group are owed $360, you'll get 67 cents on the dollar.)
>
> You may not think that they will vote in favor of the plan, but I am trying to buy up as many claims as I can and I will vote in favor of it. If I get control and you still have your claims, you will get only 67 cents on the dollar.
>
> You can protect yourself from this possibility by selling me your shares at a modest premium with your obligation to sell being conditioned on others selling to me as well. If the others don't sell to me, the condition is not triggered. You will lose nothing. But if they do, I will have to buy your share and you will get more than if you did nothing.

As each creditor listens to this offer, it becomes clear that there is nothing to lose by tendering to the outsider.

Assume first that other creditors do not accept the tender offer. The outsider leaves the scene. In this event, an individual creditor's acceptance of the tender offer comes at no cost. Those who expressed a willingness to tender are left in the same position as everyone else. Eventually a plan will go forward in which the general creditors are paid in full.

But assume most do tender. In this event, it is emphatically in the interest of each individual creditor to have tendered as well. Each creditor will receive a premium over the 67 cents on the dollar it would receive if it turned down the outsider's offer. Accepting the offer produces an outcome that is not as good as being paid 100 cents on the dollar, but that is not going to happen if the others tender and allow the outsider to gain control. No matter what happens, each creditor is no worse off by tendering and could be better off. Hence, the rational strategy for each creditor is to tender, even though collectively the creditors would be better off if all refused to do so.

If the creditors could bind each other so that they act as one, they would turn down the outsider's offer. But if they cannot act collectively, then they cannot prevent the outsider from getting the firm on the cheap. The outsider can buy the business for less than it and all the creditors know that it is worth.

This is an undesirable outcome. It is not just that the outside investor enjoys a windfall at the expense of the existing investors. It is possible that the outside investor is not the one best-suited to run this business. The firm might be worth less than $360 in this investor's hands. Yet the outside investor would still go forward with this transaction. We end up in a world in which the assets are not being put to their highest-valued use.[28]

This example illustrates the two fundamental challenges that the law of corporate reorganizations continues to face. The creditors as a group cannot bargain frictionlessly with one another. Even though they are fully informed, coalition building is costly. Reorganization law can lower these costs but cannot eliminate them altogether. Equally important, the judge is not perfectly informed, and this limits the judge's ability to prevent this sort of mischief. If the judge knew the true value of the business, it would be easy to police the outsider. But in a world in which judges do not have such knowledge, they must be on the watch for behavior that is suspect. At the same time, they must ensure that their suspicions do not get the better of them and prevent

---

[28] There is a wrinkle to this example. Each of those tendering needs to account for the possibility that the vote she casts is the one at the margin that gives the outsider control. This possibility means that any given investor might not necessarily be worse off by refusing to tender. For this reason, there is technically a nontendering equilibrium in which everyone refuses to tender, but it is very fragile. With even a tiny bit of asymmetric information, it becomes extremely unlikely, especially if there are many players. See Scott Duke Kominers & E. Glen Weyl, Holdout in the Assembly of Complements: A Problem for Market Design, 102 *Am. Econ. Rev.* 360 (2012).

the trading of claims that makes the reorganization easier and leaves the creditors as a group better off.

The advantage-taking illustrated here underscores a familiar element in play that we have seen before. The outsider is able to prevail because of a deal struck with someone who possessed control over the process. In this example, the old manager's control over the plan process was the critical lever. The outsider gained control over the manager by offering a generous consulting fee. It is cut from the same cloth as Robert Morris's side deal with the Dutch investors or the secured creditors' bargain with the shareholders in *Howard*. Judges must police against this sort of behavior as well.

The reorganization of the hotel in *Waco* reached the appellate court just as Douglas, then at the SEC, was shepherding the Chandler Act through Congress. Douglas ensured that a specific provision was added to the law that explicitly gave the judge the power to disqualify (or "designate," to use the Bankruptcy Code's language) votes cast in bad faith, in order to overrule a case like *Waco*.[29]

For Douglas, this provision merely reaffirmed that judges had a power he thought they already possessed by virtue of the Statute of 13 Elizabeth and that extended far beyond the ability to disqualify votes. Judges could do whatever was necessary to ensure that parties bargained in good faith and to protect the integrity of the process. Douglas reaffirmed this principle many times while he was serving on the Supreme Court.

The duties of everyone participating in a reorganization begin with an obligation to disclose. Parties who keep parts of any deal hidden do so at their peril, whether or not there is an explicit statutory mandate for such disclosure. But as important, the judge's police power also includes the ability to impose limits on what might be entirely innocent behavior if it reduces the risk of mischief that the judge cannot see or perhaps cannot understand. One of the most conspicuous signals that mischief might be afoot arises when one investor receives better treatment than others similarly situated. Judges do not have to bless

---

[29] Ch. X, Art. IX, §203, 52 Stat. 894. See also Ch. X, Art. VI, §146, 52 Stat. 887 (describing the "good faith" standard).

a bargain merely because it is hard to point to any specific provision of the written law that has been violated.

Young v. Higbee, another case that came before the Supreme Court in the wake of the Chandler Act, illustrates this power of the judge to exercise oversight.[30] The Higbee Company was Cleveland's great department store. Founded in 1860, Higbee was acquired in 1929 by two decidedly eccentric entrepreneurs, the Van Sweringen brothers, named Oris Paxton and Mantis James respectively. They developed Shaker Heights, among other projects. They were also, for a time, railroad tycoons. When their empire collapsed during the Great Depression, the Higbee department store was brought down along with everything else.

Charles Bradley and John Murphy, two businessmen who had served as directors of Higbee, devised a plan to rescue the company. They acquired all the junior debt of the company for less than a third of its face amount. They then proposed a plan of reorganization that would keep the preferred shareholders in place but would give themselves, in addition to a note for the amount they paid for the debt, a substantial block of common stock.

Two disgruntled preferred shareholders objected. They asserted that, because Bradley and Murphy were insiders, the debt of the reorganized firm should be subordinated to their rights as preferred shareholders. Their complaints had little merit. To be sure, there is always a risk of self-dealing when insiders are also creditors. But Bradley and Murphy were not extracting value from the business at the expense of the preferred shareholders. They were to receive under the plan notes equal to what they paid for the debt. The only possibility that they could profit came from the common stock they received under the plan. As common stock is lower in priority than the preferred stock, any return they received on their investment could not come at the expense of the preferreds.

Everything suggests this was a case in which Bradley and Murphy were simply doing their best to keep a failing business afloat during the Great Depression. There was no taking advantage of unsophisticated investors. The other parties involved were well represented (Jones Day

---

[30] 324 U.S. 204 (1945).

represented the debtor; Baker Hostetler represented J. P. Morgan). The SEC was actively involved in the case, and it approved the plan. The district court confirmed it.

The two unhappy preferred shareholders continued to make noise until Bradley and Murphy bought their shares at a premium. Bradley and Murphy were not able to rest comfortably, however. At this point, Young, another preferred shareholder, demanded that Bradley and Murphy have Higbee retain counsel and recapture the premium they had paid to the two preferred shareholders and redistribute it among all the preferred shareholders.

This case reached the Supreme Court, and it found in favor of Young. In the Supreme Court's view, the two unhappy shareholders had no obligation to continue their fight against Bradley and Murphy, but they could not use their ability to fight to obtain better treatment for themselves. Once they asserted their rights as preferred shareholders, they had a duty to act on behalf of those similarly situated: "This control of the common rights of all the preferred stockholders imposed on [them] a duty fairly to represent those common rights."[31] They were in the same position as majority shareholders who have a duty to attend to the interests of the minority shareholders.

There was some virtue in deciding the case in this fashion. Courts generally have no objection when a claims-acquirer is willing to buy out everyone in the class on the same terms. But an investor thwarts the bankruptcy process if it acts in a way that seeks to gain for itself better treatment than others similarly situated. Curbing such behavior can help ensure consensus-building within each class of similarly situated investors. By accepting a higher payment, would-be dissenters are not acting in a way that they think maximizes the value of the firm or their investment in the firm. Instead, these investors are merely trying to secure for themselves better treatment than others in their class will receive.

The ban on taking advantage of others similarly situated falls short of imposing a full-fledged fiduciary duty, and the legacy of *Young v. Higbee* remains unclear. Nevertheless, checking such behavior, even when it is not particularly malicious, underscores the constraints that the judge can place on naked self-interested bargaining in a reorganization.

---

[31] 324 U.S. at 212.

It is a mistake, however, to infer Bradley and Murphy misbehaved merely from the fact that they were willing to pay a premium for someone's shares. The opinion in *Young v. Higbee* is to some extent tone-deaf. The Court did not appear to understand that Bradley and Murphy were the good guys in the story. They rescued Higbee, and as a result the business flourished for many years thereafter. Higbee's grand Art Deco flagship store became the iconic department store. It was prominently featured in the holiday classic *A Christmas Story*.

A plan proponent may need to buy peace when someone is merely making a nuisance of themselves. There are other possibilities as well. An outsider may seek to buy claims in a class because it sees it as a good investment. The outsider may be indifferent as to who among the existing class members sells their claims. Those doing the selling to the outsider are not trying to extract value. They are simply selling their stake to someone who values it more than they do. The buyer of the claim replaces the seller of the claim in the class. From this perspective, there is no violation of the pro rata sharing norm. The buyer of the claim is the one who participates in the distribution and who will receive under the plan exactly what everyone else receives.

Another sort of issue arises when someone is willing to buy out an entire class at an amount that exceeds the payment the class will receive in the reorganization plan that is on the table. The willingness to pay more for a class of claims than the class will receive in the reorganization may itself be evidence that process itself is being hijacked. Why would an investor pay more for a claim than what it will receive under the plan unless it is getting a benefit someplace else? Why is that not like buying a dollar bill for $1.01? How can the investor vindicate its substantive rights as a holder of a claim if the investor is paying more for the claim than it will recover in the reorganization?

There are some circumstances under which someone will acquire a claim because the claim will enhance the power that person will be able to exercise in the reorganization. A substantial stakeholder may be willing to buy additional claims in the same class at a premium to ensure that a plan is defeated. The stakeholder might believe that the proposed plan puts the debtor on the wrong path. If the plan contemplates the sale of the business to someone who will not be able to run it effectively, an existing stakeholder may buy claims to vote against the plan and ensure that a different course is charted for the business. Such an investor is purchasing claims to protect the value of the firm, as this investor sees it.[32] This is unobjectionable. Of course, this claims buyer may misperceive the interests of the class, but so might anyone else.

Some resist the idea that players should be able to buy claims in order to ensure that a plan is accepted or rejected. Purchasing a claim for this purpose seems to some to be indistinguishable from buying a vote in a municipal election. While you can try to persuade voters that you are the better candidate, you cannot pay them to vote for you. If a plan is a bad idea, you can tell other stakeholders why, but you cannot buy their assent. The analogy to vote-buying in an election, however, is not entirely apt. In a reorganization, the vote is tied to ownership of the underlying asset. The two are transferred together.

Someone who buys a valuable painting buys the "vote" about how the painting is best used. It seems unobjectionable that, when someone acquires an asset, that person should be able to decide how to use it. Buying an ownership interest in a firm and the ownership rights that come with it may not be any different from buying any other asset and exercising the ownership rights that accompany it.

It is somewhat more complicated than this, of course. When the plan gives the equity of the reorganized firm to those who hold claims in a particular class, those who hold those claims know they will ultimately become the equityholders of the reorganized firm and holders of the control rights that come with equity. Control has value over and above the value of a discrete claim. This issue arises in corporate law in the context of hostile takeovers. An outsider buys stock, not as a passive investor, but to exercise rights over the firm. Judges that interpret the legacy of William O. Douglas most expansively may believe that they should police such exercises of control as part of their oversight of the bargaining process.

Douglas's conviction that the principles derived from fraudulent conveyance law empowered the judge to scrutinize the reorganization bargain sounds a new and strikingly different chord. Lawyers like Victor Morawetz did not think that judges should do more than ensure

---

[32] The court found such a purchase of claims unobjectionable in In re Pine Hill Collieries Co., 46 F. Supp. 669 (E.D. Pa. 1942).

that there was no deceit or underhanded dealing by the debtor. For them, *Boyd* did no more than ensure that everyone had a seat at the table. For Henry Hirshberg and the credit men, the judge just needed to ensure that the debtor and local creditors were not taking advantage of those who were more distant and dispersed. Paul King and the National Bankruptcy Conference wanted the judge to ensure that those involved with the bankruptcy process could bargain honestly and professionally, but again did not want them to do more. As different as Morawetz, Hirshberg, and King were from each other, all wanted a process in which the parties themselves shaped their own destiny.

By contrast, William O. Douglas and his fellow New Dealers had confidence in the ability of the judge to understand what was happening and shape the process accordingly. They believed that judges should be able to grip the reins of the reorganization process tightly. The judge had to apply the principles of the Statute of 13 Elizabeth with a heavy hand, insist on full disclosure, and be quick to act whenever there was potential for advantage-taking. Those who negotiated with one another in a corporate reorganization could not be completely trusted to bargain in a way such that everyone's interest was protected. In the case of the reorganization of large firms, judges had to be especially alert to those with knowledge from profiting at the expense of the unsophisticated.

The role of the judge became much greater in the wake of Douglas's reforms. It is important to remember, however, that the principles that guide the judge were still centered on the idea that creditors should not be able to manipulate legal processes to their own advantage. The judge's power derived from the same principles that were at work in a nascent form in the case of Blair McClenachan

The inherent power of the judge to oversee the reorganization was only part of the reforms that Douglas brought to the law while he sat on the Supreme Court. To a much greater extent than judges before or since, Douglas believed that these powers served in the first instance to protect the substantive entitlements of the stakeholders, and he had strong views about what these substantive rights were. The next chapter focuses on his conception of these substantive rights, a conception that cast a long shadow over the written and unwritten rules of modern reorganization law.

5   PRIORITY MATTERS

One of the great debates in the legal academy during the 1930s was over the way a reorganization affected the rights of senior and junior investors. At loggerheads were the usual suspects. In one camp were the investment bankers and their lawyers, most conspicuously Robert Swaine. They favored what came to be called relative priority. In the other camp were the New Deal reformers, most conspicuously, Jerome Frank and William O. Douglas. They favored absolute priority. The following hypothetical example illustrates the difference between these two priority regimes.

Imagine a firm has only one project and two investors. At the outset, the two investors agree that one investor will be entitled to $150 when the project is completed and the other will be entitled to whatever remains. Their lawyers implement this deal by giving a $150 debt instrument to the first investor and equity to the second. Time passes, and it becomes clear that the project will yield either $200 or $0 with equal probability. At this point, a government regulation unexpectedly requires the firm to eliminate all debt in its capital structure. A market sale is not in the collective interest of the two investors. No outsider is willing to pay anything close to the firm's expected value.

Because the two investors can realize value from their investment only by putting a new capital structure in place, it is in their joint interest to do so. How should the securities in the reorganized firm be divided between the senior and the junior investor? Upon what allocation rule would the parties have agreed had they thought about the need for such a restructuring at the time of their original investment?

There are two equally sensible ways of thinking about the question. One is relative priority. Before the need for restructuring arose, the senior investor had an equal chance of being paid $0 or $150. Its investment had a present value of $75. The junior investor had an equal chance of receiving $0 or $50 (the amount left over if the project is successful, and the other investor is paid $150). This was worth $25. By this logic, the most sensible division of value would be one that gave 75 percent to the senior investor and 25 percent to the junior investor. There is no reason for the external regulation that required eliminating debt to change the value of the stake each had in the venture at the time of the restructuring.

The possibility that the project might ultimately be worth more than what is owed the senior investor gave option value to the junior investor's stake before the regulation. A rational investor would have been willing to pay $25 for the stake, as it was the equivalent of an option to acquire the project in a year from the senior investor in exchange for $150. The project will fail half the time, and the option is worthless. In that case, the holder of the option walks away with nothing. But when the project succeeds, the investor holding the option exercises it and enjoys the $50 of value that remains after the senior investor is paid off.

The alternative to relative priority is absolute priority. Under this conception of priority, the restructuring is a day of reckoning. All future possibilities are collapsed to the present. The project has an expected value of $100, reflecting the equal chance that it will be worth $200 or $0. Even if the firm could be sold today for what it was worth, no buyer would pay more than this amount. This is less than the $150 that the senior investor is owed. Hence, the senior investor should receive 100 percent of the project, and the junior investor should receive nothing.

Options are a component of every investment instrument. Whenever one investor has priority over another, the junior investor has what is in effect a call option. The junior investor has the ability, set out in the investment instrument, to terminate the senior investor's rights by paying the investor off. This call option is the right to buy a particular position for a fixed price at a particular time. It is defined by a strike price and an exercise date. In this hypothetical, the strike price is simply the amount owed the senior investor. The exercise date sets the time when the holder of the option must decide whether to exercise the option. This hypothetical raises the question whether the regulation that requires the elimination of debt advances the exercise date of the junior investor's option to acquire the senior investor's position for $150.

The essential difference between absolute and relative priority is the effect that entry into a reorganization has on the exercise date of the call-option component of the junior investment instrument. Absolute priority accelerates the exercise date; a regime of relative priority leaves it untouched. To return to the hypothetical, the difference between priority regimes lies in whether the junior investor has to pay off the senior investor (that is, whether the junior investor is forced to exercise its option to buy out the senior investor for $150) at the time the firm receives a new capital structure (absolute priority) or whether the junior investor can wait until after the project is over before deciding to pay off the senior investor (relative priority).

Reorganization professionals today enjoyed educations that included the lessons of modern finance. They have little trouble articulating the difference between relative and absolute priority. Indeed, it is hard for them to think about priority without using the language of options. Swaine and Frank, however, took the debate stage decades before Franco Modigliani and Merton Miller.[1] The language of options was not available to them. Each had trouble justifying his own position and understanding that of the other.

They attempted to set out the contours of the debate in a series of law review articles featuring Robert Swaine and Jerome Frank respectively. To contemporary readers, neither distinguished himself. They spent much of their time talking past each other.

Swaine did not see any need to justify relative priority in a rigorous fashion. In his view, the role of the law was not to enforce any particular priority regime, but rather to allow the investment bankers to bring

---

[1] Modigliani and Miller showed that if one makes only a few assumptions, capital structure has no effect on firm value. See Franco Modigliani & Merton Miller, The Cost of Capital, Corporation Finance and the Theory of Investment, 48 *Am. Econ. Rev.* 261 (1958). Much of finance ever since has focused on how these assumptions (or irrelevance axioms, as they are called) might not apply in practice. They allow for discussion of differences across priority regimes to be done with formal rigor.

about a successful reorganization. Such a reorganization was one that satisfied their clients and induced them to part with their capital in new ventures even after some failed. Swaine did little more than assert that the norms of the investment bankers produced good outcomes over the mine-run of cases. He appeared entirely too comfortable with the status quo.

Swaine would have strengthened his argument considerably if he had at least identified the core rationale for relative priority. Preserving relative priority ensured an outcome in an equity receivership that was the same as what would happen in an exchange offer outside of a reorganization. Each investor received a new security that had a value more or less equal to the one each was giving up. Even though the security took an entirely different form and contained a different package of rights, it was worth roughly the same as (or perhaps worth a little more than) the one the investor had possessed before. Hence, there were few fights over value. Moreover, by maintaining the relative value of each party's stake in the venture, the stakeholders are all more likely to focus upon maximizing the value of the venture as a whole.

The New Deal reformers never took relative priority seriously. It never occurred to them to ask whether the priority regime that the norms of investment bankers embodied promoted bargaining. They failed to understand how reputational forces during this era might have kept the greed and self-interest of the investment bankers in check. They did not understand that a central tenet of their critique of equity receiverships – that insiders and the professionals who represented them profited at the expense of those who held senior bonds – was suspect.

If investment bankers routinely stole from their clients in the event of a reorganization, these clients should anticipate the losses they would suffer and demand a return at the outset that compensated them. In well-functioning capital markets, outsiders receive a competitive return on their investments. As an empirical matter, this proved to be the case for these senior securities over this time period.[2] Frank and Douglas

---

[2] During this era, those who held diversified portfolios of senior securities in large firms enjoyed at least the market return on their investments. See W. Braddock Hickman, *Corporate Bond Quality and Investor Experience* 338, 509 (Princeton University Press, 1958).

asserted outsider investors were being systematically short-changed. This was an empirical claim, and it turned out to be false.

There was also a failure of imagination on the part of Jerome Frank and William O. Douglas. They thought that absolute priority followed from the nature of the legal procedure on which the equity receivership rested. In an actual foreclosure sale, creditors are lined up in order of seniority and the debtor stands last in line. Cash proceeds are distributed first to the most senior creditors. Only after they are paid in full do the junior creditors receive anything, and only if they are paid in full does anything go to the debtor. The New Dealers did not think a coherent restructuring regime that took the same form could be any different. Even though no one thought that the foreclosure sale in an equity receivership was anything more than a legal fiction, Frank and Douglas simply assumed that the priority consequences for a virtual sale had to be the same as for an actual one. The consequences *could* be the same, of course, but it was not logically necessary.

If the New Deal reformers had the benefit of the intuitions of modern finance, they might have been able to see that a reorganization does not logically require accelerating the exercise date embedded in junior instruments. But they would likely have resisted this intellectual leap in any event. Compared with the rigid system of priority that would follow from a foreclosure sale, the norms of investment bankers tended to shift value away from outside public investors who held senior debt instruments to insiders who held equity. This seemed suspect on its own terms.

Of course, again with the benefit of modern finance, greater returns ex post for more senior investors is beside the point. To be sure, to the extent that senior investors find themselves in a relative priority world, they need a higher interest rate to give them a market return on their capital and junior investors need a correspondingly lower one. But all investors in equilibrium should get the market return on their capital. Relative priority carves up the pie differently than absolute priority, but, without more, one cannot say whether it increases or reduces the size of the pie.

Nor does one priority regime or the other exacerbate the problem of financial distress. Financial distress arises because of other features of investment instruments. Investment instruments contain rights to some of the firm's cashflows. A shareholder receives dividends; a debtholder is entitled to the repayment of principal and interest on a fixed schedule. Financial distress arises because of the inability of the debtor to satisfy the cashflow rights of the investors.

Investment instruments also embody control rights. These too affect how financial distress plays itself out. Shareholders enjoy control rights directly. They have voting rights. They elect the board of directors. Creditors also enjoy control rights. Even when the firm is enjoying the sunniest of times, the debtor often needs permission from its lead lender to make major capital investments or take on additional debt. As the firm falls deeper into financial distress, it becomes increasingly likely that it will breach one or more covenants.

The breach itself might not be of great moment. For example, it may be nothing more than a delay in filing a financial report, but the breach is a default nevertheless, and it gives a creditor the power to terminate its loan. Creditors are usually willing to waive defaults, but they subject their waivers to conditions. Enormous creditor control comes from their ability to impose these conditions, especially when the debtor has entered choppy waters and cannot find someone else to make a replacement loan on terms that are as favorable.

Financial distress often requires altering the cashflow and control rights of junior investors. Indeed, cashflow and control rights are the principal drivers of financial distress. When a firm may not even be able to pay its senior creditors, it may no longer be sensible for junior stakeholders to call the shots or enjoy interest payments and dividends. They are no longer the residual owners of the firm who enjoy the benefit of each marginal dollar the firm gains and suffer the cost of each one it loses.

But neither cashflow nor control rights are relevant to the choice between absolute and relative priority. Priority is about what each investor receives at the end of the day when all accounts are squared. The firm continues to exist until senior investors seize the assets and sell them. As long as the firm continues, there is no need to square the accounts, no matter how financially distressed the firm might be. The ultimate allocation of firm value between junior and senior investors can be put off. In the case of the AT&SF, the senior investors had to wait a hundred years for their principal. It is possible to fix the rights of junior and senior investors at the time of the restructuring as absolute priority does, but it is not necessary to do so.

Consistent with the modest role that Swaine saw for the judge, relative priority can be implemented without the need for a judge to value the firm. For example, the senior investor can be given all the equity in the reorganized firm, and the junior investor can be given a call option on this equity with a strike price equal to the amount owed the senior investor. The cashflow and control rights of the junior investor can be scaled back (or even eliminated) so as not to interfere with the operation of the business. The senior investor will be paid first when the firm is ultimately sold or wrapped up. But the junior investor still receives its share if any money is left over at that time.

Implementing absolute priority in a reorganization requires knowing the value of the firm. The example offered at the beginning of this chapter assumed that the project had a fifty-fifty chance of being worth $200 or nothing, and hence it was worth $100. But the value of a firm is rarely clear. It is a guess compounded by an estimate.[3] Under absolute priority, the judge cannot confirm a plan that wipes out the junior investor without concluding that the firm is worth less than the senior investor is owed. Absolute priority, by its nature, requires assessing the value of the firm against the amount owed the senior investor. This is easy enough when there is an actual sale in a liquid market, but not otherwise.

Frank and Douglas believed judges could put a value on firms, but they did not squarely confront the problems that necessarily arise when uncertainty makes a huge range of valuations possible in every case. A rule that mandates absolute priority in a reorganization vindicates it in a particular case only if the judge can value the business accurately. Under absolute priority, it takes only slight changes in the value of the firm for a particular tranche of debt to be paid in full or receive nothing at all. In the absence of a sale in the marketplace, absolute priority leads to valuation disputes as inexorably as night follows day.

Under relative priority, it is not necessary to know the value of the business. A call option can be given to the junior investor that has only

---

[3] This phrase is usually attributed to Peter Coogan. See Peter F. Coogan, Confirmation of a Plan Under the Bankruptcy Code, 32 *Case W. Res. L. Rev.* 301, 313 n. 62 (1982) (tracing the attribution of the phrase).

two components: the strike price and an exercise date. Neither requires knowing anything about the value of the firm. When implementing relative priority, the judge needs to know only how much the senior lender is owed and the ultimate date on which accounts must be settled. (These are the strike price and the exercise date of the option, respectively.)

Nor was it of great moment during the era of equity receiverships that relative priority was implemented with junior securities rather than call options. As long as investment bankers were honest brokers and as long as investors held diversified portfolios, it did not matter that relative priority was implemented only approximately. A stakeholder who received a bit too much in one case would receive a bit too little in the next. The principal virtue of relative priority was that its distributional scheme caused little disruption and minimized fights among the players.

New Deal reformers gravitated toward absolute priority not merely because they were chained to the form of the foreclosure sale. They also had confidence in judges. They trusted in the ability of judges to meet the technical challenge of asset valuation. Once one assumed judges could meet the challenge of valuing a firm, the rigidity of absolute priority has a distinct appeal for anyone concerned, as Frank and Douglas were, about the possibility of advantage-taking. When investment bankers and their professionals ran reorganizations, they could lowball small investors. To guard against such abuses, the substantive rights of the senior creditors had to be easy to understand, and absolute priority is the most straightforward of rules.

Moreover, absolutely priority is particularly valuable to a risk-averse investor who is not diversified. Ordinarily, an investor who holds a diversified portfolio is indifferent between a security with a low rate of interest under a regime of absolute priority and the same security with a higher rate of interest under a regime of relative priority. The higher interest rate in good states of the world compensates for greater losses in bad states. When an investor holds a large bundle of securities, the higher interest rate on the securities that pay off will make up for the few that default. The returns from the portfolio as a whole will be the same.

But small investors in the first half of the twentieth century did not hold diversified portfolios.[4] Bonds were bought in units of $1,000, and many small investors owned bonds of only a few firms. The failure of any given firm had momentous consequences. Given their lack of diversification, small individual investors were better off holding the most senior instruments with the strongest priority rights.

The value of a senior instrument is subject to less variance. If a firm is worth $100, an undiversified investor would much rather have a senior security estimated to be worth $50 than a piece of equity estimated to be worth $50. New Deal reformers may have intuited this idea, albeit imperfectly. While on the Court, Douglas insisted that an investor who held senior bonds could not be forced to take junior bonds of the same value without being given a "bonus" to make up for taking securities of an inferior grade. Justice Douglas explained this in *Consolidated Rock Products Co. v. Du Bois*: "[W]hile creditors may be given inferior grades of securities, their 'superior rights' must be recognized. Clearly, those prior rights are not recognized ... if creditors are given only a face amount of inferior securities equal to the face amount of their claims. They must receive, in addition, compensation for the senior rights which they are to surrender."[5]

It might be that Justice Douglas was asserting that a bond backed by collateral is inherently worth more than a share of stock that trades for the same price because one is backed by a hard asset with a certain value, and the other is not. As between a bond that trades for $100 and a share of stock that trades for $100, one always prefers the former because the return is more certain. A bond is inherently worth more than a share of stock of equal value for the same reason that a pound of lead weighs more than a pound of feathers.

But there is a chance that the conclusion that Douglas reached rested on an intuition that was not quite so silly. If risk-averse investors

---

[4] Brian Boessenecker has identified the difficulties small investors faced in holding a diversified portfolio in the first half of the twentieth century and their implications for priority rules. There is another problem that Boessenecker also identifies. A substantial part of the market consisted of distressed bonds acquired in the wake of a reorganization. Acquiring these bonds (given the hurdles one needed to go through and the extra capital one needed to put up) was easier for more sophisticated investors.

[5] Consolidated Rock Products Co. v. Du Bois, 312 U.S. 510, 528–29 (1941).

are undiversified, they are worse off with junior securities, all else equal, because the value of junior securities is subject to greater variance.

The New Deal reformers believed that absolute priority was an important protection for small investors who held senior securities in a firm that was being reorganized, but nothing in the Chandler Act or earlier law explicitly required absolute priority. The Chandler Act, like §77B, required only that the plan be "fair and equitable." Courts used the phrase "fair and equitable" and similar language in *Paton*, *Monon*, and *Boyd* in the course of answering the question of what kind of scrutiny the court should give the reorganization process. These cases were about giving everyone a seat at the table, not about priority rights. Whether a plan was "fair and equitable" turned on the process that led to agreement on the plan of reorganization, not its content.

But while at the SEC, Frank and Douglas sought to change this understanding of "fair and equitable" and transform it into a priority rule. They tried to persuade courts that "fair and equitable" went beyond process and incorporated a right of each senior creditor to insist on absolute priority. They found a suitable case in which to raise the issue. The lawyers at the SEC filed an amicus brief in this case with the Supreme Court. They couched their argument in this fashion:

> This Court has several times declared that the condition of participation by junior interests in a reorganization plan is the prior satisfaction of all senior claims. This has been called the doctrine of "absolute priority." ... [N]o deviation from this principle of fairness has appeared in the decisions of this Court, and very little express deviation from it is apparent in decisions of the lower courts. However, while paying lip service to the rule, the lower courts have at times exhibited a tendency to sanction plans which circumvent the rule.[6]

This argument is, of course, disingenuous. In its earlier cases, the Court had not specified what constituted "satisfaction" of a senior claim. The opinions were consistent with the idea that the senior creditors had to be paid in full, as absolute priority required, but the

---

[6] Brief for the United States Amicus Curiae at 13–14, Case v. Los Angeles Lumber Products Co., 308 U.S. 106 (1939).

opinions were also consistent with the idea that senior creditors could be "satisfied" with only the share to which relative priority entitled them. It would have been equally accurate to have asserted that no deviation from relative priority had appeared in the Court's decisions and that lower courts, to the extent that they had confronted the question, tended to favor relative over absolute priority.

Lawyers at the SEC were confident its argument would find a sympathetic ear. As the case moved through the lower courts, William O. Douglas had himself moved from the SEC to the Supreme Court. After he read the petition asking the Supreme Court to resolve the question, he pushed his colleagues on the Court to hear the case, and they were willing to defer to his expertise when it came to deciding the merits. After all, he had been a professor at the Yale Law School who specialized in corporate reorganizations. He must know the law.

The case was *Case v. Los Angeles Lumber Products*, and it was one of the first that Justice Douglas heard on the Court.[7] The narrow question was the meaning of "fair and equitable." The phrase appeared in §77B, the reorganization statutory regime enacted in 1934, as well as in Chapter XI and Chapter X. There was no evidence that the phrase was intended to do more than embody the principle that entitled everyone to a right to participate in the bargaining as *Boyd* required. Douglas, however, used this case as a vehicle to inject a substantive right into the fair and equitable test.

Los Angeles Lumber Products began as a shipyard that built ships for the navy during the Great War.[8] After the war ended, the demand for ships fell. The owners of the shipyard sought to change course and use their facilities to take advantage of the building boom in Los Angeles during the 1920s.

They believed that they could transport raw lumber from the Pacific Northwest to Los Angeles by water and finish it in new facilities they

---

[7] This case arose under §77B, but because it required interpreting the words "fair and equitable," and the same words appeared in Chapter X, whatever gloss given to the phrase in that case would apply equally in Chapter X.

[8] The definitive account of the case and its background can be found in a splendid piece by Robert Rasmussen. See Robert K. Rasmussen, The Story of *Case v. Los Angeles Lumber Products*: Old Equity Holders and the Reorganized Corporation, *Bankruptcy Law Stories* 157–58 (Foundation Press 2007). The details presented here are drawn from his account.

built at the harbor. By taking advantage of the lower costs of water transport, they would gain a competitive advantage over those who brought finished lumber from the Northwest by rail. The new lumber business would buttress the largely moribund shipbuilding business.

Believing their future lay with lumber rather than shipbuilding, they renamed their firm Los Angeles Lumber Products. But things did not work out as planned. Among other difficulties, the firm needed to transport the finished lumber a short distance by rail, and rail rates were regulated. The railroads that carried lumber from the Pacific Northwest persuaded the regulators to set the rates for transporting lumber from Los Angeles harbor high enough to render Los Angeles Lumber Products uncompetitive.

The lumber business failed after two years. Still called Los Angeles Lumber Products, the firm returned to shipbuilding. There were few navy ships to be built during this period, and Los Angeles Lumber still had to service debt from the failed lumber business. This it could not do, and it was forced to restructure its debts outside of bankruptcy in 1930. Circumstances made a consensual deal possible. California was late in providing limited liability to those who did business in corporate form, and the old equity investors were willing to see a considerable dilution of their stake in the firm to ensure that their liability was limited. As part of the deal, the bondholders agreed that interest was to be payable only as earned.

The shipyard continued to struggle during the 1930s, but then military spending slowly began to increase as war clouds gathered. In order to be competitive, however, Los Angeles Lumber needed to modernize its equipment. This required new capital, but no one wanted to invest in Los Angeles Lumber given that there were already senior creditors entitled to be paid first.

There was a second and even bigger problem. The navy required its shipbuilders to find a surety, someone willing to commit to finishing the job if the prime contractor failed. A surety has to be able to access a firm's assets if it is called upon to finish a job, and it cannot do this if a senior creditor can foreclose on them. No one was going to give a surety bond to Los Angeles Lumber Products with the senior debt it carried. To find a surety, Los Angeles Lumber had to reduce its debt dramatically.

While all of this was going on, the senior creditors had no power to foreclose and acquire the business for themselves. Given the terms of the workout in 1930, in the absence of any earnings the senior creditors were owed nothing until their bonds became due in 1944. There was no default, and the senior creditors had no way to force out the equity-holders who controlled the firm. Nor did they want to. The financial distress the firm faced in 1937 was not the result of bad performance. Nothing suggested that anything was amiss with the way the business was being run. Indeed, the shareholders and the control they exercised over the business brought value.

The old directors and the old shareholders who were controlling the business went to the bondholders and proposed a restructuring under §77B. They suggested that the bondholders trade their debt for equity. If this were done, there would be lucrative government contracts. These would probably not be enough to repay them in full, but it was the only way they would enjoy a substantial return. It is worth noting – and this was not uncommon – that the largest shareholder also controlled one of the largest bondholders. This made the challenge of finding consensus easier. Ninety percent of the bondholders eventually agreed to the shareholders' plan.

In the restructuring, the old bondholders would receive most of the equity, and the old shareholders would retain only a sliver. The existing directors would stay in place. Los Angeles Lumber would go forward and try to land navy contracts. In all likelihood, of course, the equity of the bondholders would never be worth as much as they were owed. But if there were a war on a scale never seen before, the bondholders might receive even more. Most important, regardless of what the future held, doing nothing spelled certain failure for the business, while a reorganization would allow the business to focus on supplying a product (navy ships) for which there was a growing demand.

The reorganization plan did not respect absolute priority, as the equityholders would remain in the picture even though the shipyard, even if successfully reorganized, was worth in expectation less than the senior creditors were owed. Nevertheless, the reorganization would leave the bondholders better off than if there were no reorganization at all. The value of their stake would go up in the wake of a reorganization. An investor would rather have most of the equity in a company that has a decent chance of landing lucrative shipbuilding contracts than a bond in a company that has no chance of getting them.

The proponents of the plan in *Los Angeles Lumber* argued that the plan was "fair and equitable" as §77B required. Courts, such as the one in *Paton*, used the term "fair and equitable" to ensure that the reorganization possessed no badges of fraud, and there were none here. There was no failure of process. Everyone had a seat at the table, and the new securities the bondholders received were worth more than the ones they were giving up. Moreover, there was no advantage-taking of innocent outsiders. The investors were all well informed and sophisticated.

But two bondholders, Thomas Case and Adele Cowan, dissented. No one was denying them the ability to participate fully in the process. There were no side deals. Nothing was hidden. The plan provided each creditor with exactly the same treatment as other, similarly situated creditors. Nor were Case and Cowan babes in the woods. They were distressed debt investors who bought their bonds at substantial discounts, and they likely did so in order to shake down everyone else.

The lawyers at the SEC argued that absent a waiver on their part, Case and Cowan had the right to be paid in full before the shareholders could receive anything. "Fair and equitable," they urged, meant more than having a seat at the bargaining table. Even though the bonds were not in default, the reorganization created a day of reckoning, and in any such reckoning, senior bondholders were entitled to be paid in full before anyone junior was paid a penny. As long as they refused to give their consent, Case and Cowan were entitled to be paid 100 cents on the dollar before the shareholders received anything.

From the perspective of New Deal reformers, a majority of bondholders should not be able to agree to reduce principal or interest payments under a bond indenture unilaterally. Any change had to be made in a bankruptcy restructuring overseen by a judge in which everyone had the ability to stand by their rights. An investor could waive absolute priority, but the choice remained with the investor.

The lawyers at the SEC understood, of course, that Case and Cowan were vulture investors, but they wanted to establish absolute priority as the principle that governed the reorganization of large firms. Giving each senior investor the right to insist on being paid in full offered protection against insiders who controlled the reorganization process and might abuse their power.

Giving everyone such a veto, of course, did create the risk of holdouts, but the New Deal reformers downplayed this risk. They believed that the judge could police against misbehavior. If Case and Cowan were acting in bad faith, the Chandler Act gave the judge the power to deal with it. Among other things, the judge might designate their vote. But the other creditors had to show Case and Cowan were violating the principles of the Statute of 13 Elizabeth. In the absence of such a showing, they were entitled to insist on absolute priority.

That absolute priority introduced valuation uncertainties was not itself troubling to the reformers either. Under Chapter X, an independently appointed trustee crafted the plan, and the SEC and the judge had to approve it. What motivated the New Deal reformers in the first instance was ensuring that outsiders were protected against investment bankers and corporate insiders. As long as those doing the valuation were alert to the need to protect small investors, the imprecision that came with it was not of great moment. Indeed, as we shall see in the next chapter, this same uncertainty allowed judges to put a thumb on the scale when large financial institutions were senior in the capital structure and those needing protection were junior.

After Thomas Case's victory in the Supreme Court, the workers at the shipyard passed the hat among themselves. They raised $28,000, and they tried to buy Case out for this amount, but Case rejected their offer. He insisted on being paid the full $35,000 he was owed. He was not called out for engaging in hold-up behavior. A plan was eventually put in place that shut out the old equityholders. But without them the shipyard failed, even after a world war broke out. Los Angeles Lumber Products floundered and was soon absorbed into another firm.

The fate of Los Angeles Lumber Products after the Supreme Court rejected its reorganization plan proved a harbinger of the unhappy fate awaiting other firms that entered Chapter X. *Los Angeles Lumber*'s interpretation of "fair and equitable" came just after Chapter X was enacted. Another of Chapter X's reforms was the prohibition of investment bankers who had been involved with the issuance of the bonds from taking part in any later restructuring of the firm. The control over the reorganization process passed from investment bankers to a bureaucracy inside the SEC. This small fiefdom was not accountable to anyone and took much too long to resolve cases. It became nearly impossible to reorganize a firm where the old shareholders had expertise essential to the success of the business.

Excluding investment bankers from reorganization practice affected corporate reorganizations in another way. These investment bankers were the clients of Paul Cravath and Robert Swaine and other Wall Street lawyers. Excluding investment bankers from corporate reorganizations meant that Cravath, Swaine, and other Wall Street lawyers abandoned reorganization practice.

New Deal lawyers departed too. Jerome Frank and William O. Douglas left the orbit of corporate reorganizations and ended up on the bench, as did Henry Friendly. Thurmond Arnold, after a short stint on the bench, flourished in a law practice based in Washington that focused on administrative law. Abe Fortas joined him until he was appointed to the Supreme Court. Others, such as Lloyd Cutler, Homer Kripke, and Edward Levi, pursued careers in government and the academy.

As a result, the professionals in reorganization practice who remained were the lawyers who represented the credit men in small bankruptcies. Future reforms of reorganization law fell into the hands of Paul King's successors. They were the ones to emerge from the contest among the three contending forces that had embarked on reorganization reform at the start of the 1930s, and they were the only group that had no strong ideological commitment to either absolute or relative priority. They cared only that square corners were cut and that neither the debtor nor noncooperative creditors engaged in last-minute manipulations or advantage-taking.

Chapter XI had the same "fair and equitable" language as Chapter X. As a result, if lower courts read *Los Angeles Lumber* literally, they would have to alter the way small businesses were restructured. If each creditor were armed with such a right, each one would have the power to hold up any restructuring in which the old shareholders remained with the business. Compositions would not be possible. Everyone understood, however, that Douglas intended no such result. Neither he nor anyone else actually thought "fair and equitable" meant "absolute priority." It was just a convenient hook he used to put in place the priority regime that he thought suited large reorganizations.

Eventually, Congress dropped "fair and equitable" from Chapter XI, making it plain that dissenting creditors could not insist upon absolute priority when it came to reorganizing small businesses in Chapter XI. The regime that the credit men favored remained in place. If creditors collectively thought old shareholders running the debtor were worthy, they would give them equity in the reorganized business, but not otherwise. The creditors were in control. Shareholders had no power to remain over their objection, but as long as there was a consensus among the creditors as a group, an individual creditor could not throw a spanner in the works.

Financially distressed businesses and their creditors turned increasingly to Chapter XI. Although this reorganization regime was conceived for small businesses, nothing by its terms limited it to them. Although it provided no mechanism for restructuring secured debt, its automatic stay could at least hold these creditors at bay. Over time, as the failure of Chapter X became increasingly obvious, the firms that entered Chapter XI became increasingly large, culminating finally in 1975 with the filing of W. T. Grant, the seventeenth-largest retailer in the United States at the time with sales of $1.6 billion.

In the decades that followed the Chandler Act, the imprecision built into the absolute priority rule cast an increasingly long shadow. Judges used the uncertainty baked into the rule to exercise ever greater discretion. This discretion, however, was not used in service of policing the bargaining process, but rather to allow judges to distribute more value to junior investors when it seemed to them appropriate. The law and the language of corporate reorganizations fell out of sync with each other because judges were willing to put a thumb on the scale. The problems this created are the focus of the next chapter.

6   A THUMB ON THE SCALE

After *Los Angeles Lumber*, the letter of the law mandated absolute priority in large reorganizations, but valuation uncertainty led to something less than absolute priority on the ground. If the equityholders were small investors rather than insiders, judges were more inclined to put on rose-colored glasses. They would find a distressed debtor solvent and thus allow the equityholders to remain in place.

This disconnect between the language of corporate reorganizations and the law as it played out made some uneasy.[1] For the heirs of William O. Douglas, however, this was a feature, not a bug. While they gave lip-service to absolute priority, they also welcomed the license judges enjoyed to make sure the good guys won. They embraced the idea of the "worthy debtor." To the extent that giving a helping hand to worthy debtors was a sound bankruptcy policy, giving the benefit of the doubt to junior investors seemed a coherent principle, even if an unwritten one. Their intuition told them that distributions of value to junior investors were independently good, notwithstanding absolute priority.[2]

For the bankruptcy professionals who followed in the footsteps of the credit men, this state of affairs was not itself troubling. Their norms

---

[1] Most prominent of these was Walter Blum. See Walter J. Blum, The Law and Language of Corporate Reorganization, 17 *U. Chi. L. Rev.* 565 (1950). Blum, one of the giants in the mid-twentieth-century legal academy, was my colleague at the University of Chicago for many years, and it was a great privilege to be introduced to many of the mysteries of corporate reorganizations by him.

[2] Most prominent among Douglas's heirs was Vern Countryman, who served William O. Douglas as a law clerk and later taught at Yale and then Harvard. Succeeding Countryman at Harvard and possessed of similar views was Elizabeth Warren. See Elizabeth Warren, Bankruptcy Policy, 54 *U. Chi. L. Rev.* 775 (1987).

already reflected the idea of the worthy debtor and the virtues of debt rehabilitation. More to the point, they were less exposed to the hazards of judicial valuation. Theirs was primarily the world of Chapter XI and small businesses. In Chapter XI, the judge had no power to confirm a plan that the creditors, as a group, opposed. Moreover, the credit men as a group supported desirable restructurings. They were willing to take less than payment in full and leave an entrepreneur in place when they were honest and competent, and their business was cashflow-positive. They were not being altruistic. They would enjoy future business from such debtors. And when they judged a debtor unworthy, they could pull the plug, regardless of what the judge thought.

Complicating this picture, however, was the way that bankruptcy law treated real estate ventures. A real estate venture was not like a typical business. A management company ran the day-to-day operations. The venture itself had no employees, and its owners were primarily passive investors. It was apparent at the time of the Chandler Act, however, that real estate ventures could face some of the same challenges as ordinary businesses. Office buildings were sometimes housed in corporations and financed with multiple layers of bonds that were widely held. Section 77B provided an appropriate vehicle for such real estate ventures. But large buildings were not always held in corporations. When the Chandler Act was being passed in the late 1930s, it was thought sensible to offer such real estate ventures a way to restructure their debt in bankruptcy as well.

Chapter XII was added without much deliberation to the Chandler Act, and it extended the benefits of Chapter X to real estate ventures even when not housed in corporations. As originally enacted, Chapter XII, like Chapter X and Chapter XI, required that plans of reorganization be "fair and equitable." When Congress dropped the "fair and equitable" language in Chapter XI to underscore that the absolute priority rule did not apply to small businesses, it deleted this language from Chapter XII as well. Later changes also eliminated the requirement of a mandatory trustee, thus allowing the old managers to remain in place and propose a plan.[3]

---

[3] Like Chapter X, Chapter XII required the mandatory appointment of a trustee. Under the 1898 Act, however, the Bankruptcy Rules could effect a substantive change in the bankruptcy law and in 1975, the Bankruptcy Rules were amended to eliminate this requirement that a trustee be appointed in every case.

Neither of these changes might seem of great moment. Nothing in Chapter XII suggested that, in the absence of consent of creditors as a group, investors in a real estate venture had any right to participate unless the venture's creditors were paid in full. A mortgage on the real property could be modified only if the rights of the creditors holding the mortgage were "adequately protected,"[4] and courts had long held that adequate protection required giving such creditors a "substitute of the most indubitable equivalence" of their interest in the debtor's property.[5]

This conventional wisdom, however, was upended in the 1970s when the number of Chapter XII filings increased dramatically.[6] A recession hit the economy, and a large number of real estate ventures failed. These failed real estate ventures were usually cut from the same cloth. During this time, the maximum income tax rate for earned income was 50 percent, and the maximum tax rate on investment income was 70 percent. These rates gave people a strong incentive to search for ways to defer the recognition of income, and one of the best ways to defer taxation was to take advantage of the accelerated depreciation rules for investments in real property. Tax shelters structured in this fashion, however, suffered from a conspicuous weakness. They leaked.[7]

Let us assume (to keep the math simple) that an investor faces a marginal tax rate of 50 percent and there is no inflation. This investor acquires an ownership interest in Blackacre for $100. It generates no income. Let us assume that the tax rules allow an investor to depreciate the entire value of Blackacre in a single year. Let us also assume that this investor makes $100 in income from some other source. Because of the investor's ability to depreciate Blackacre, no taxes have to be paid today. There is income of $100, but ownership of Blackacre provides

---

[4] 1898 Bankruptcy Act §461(11).

[5] See In re Murel Holding Corp., 75 F.2d 941, 942 (2d Cir. 1935) (L. Hand, J.).

[6] Indeed, over 40 percent of Chapter XII filings occurred between 1974 and 1976. See Harvey R. Miller and Marcia L. Goldstein, Chapter XII – Real Property Arrangements: Is "Cram Down" a Debtor's Panacea?, 12 Real Property, Probate and Trust J. 695, 695–703 (1977).

[7] This phrase was coined by Martin Ginsburg. See Martin D. Ginsburg, The Leaky Tax Shelter, 53 Taxes 719 (1975). Ginsburg was, by common account, one of the greatest tax lawyers who ever lived. It was my great good fortune to have had him as a teacher in law school, and he remained a most generous mentor for many years thereafter.

an offsetting deduction of $100. The investor invests the income of $100 (instead of only the $50 the investor would have after taxes absent the deduction that ownership of Blackacre provided). Ten years later, the investor sells Blackacre for $100.

At this point, the investor does realize $100 of income and owes $50 of tax on it. The postponement of the tax, however, has given the investor a chance to invest the extra $50 (the amount of tax saved in the first year because of the ability to depreciate Blackacre). Instead of paying tax on income when it was earned, the investor pays the same amount ten years later after having had the chance to put the money to work in the meantime.

And this understates the tax benefits. Real estate investors – very often professionals in high-income occupations such as dentists, doctors, and lawyers – could invest in Blackacre with borrowed money and still enjoy the entire tax benefit. They could put $10 into the venture and borrow $90 against Blackacre on a nonrecourse basis and still take the $100 deduction. When Blackacre was sold, they would still have to pay tax on the full $100, but the amount for which they sold the property would be more than enough to cover the tax and over the short term they received a tax benefit that was even larger than the amount of money they put at risk in Blackacre.[8]

This ability to postpone taxes was one of the principal drivers of limited real estate partnerships. Because of the lure of tax shelters, dentists, doctors, lawyers, and others with large, earned incomes invested in them, not because they knew much about real estate, but because doing so gave them what appeared to be such an easy way to limit their taxes.

Such strategies pay off handsomely over the long run if the underlying investment proves successful. But the investors' lack of expertise and the lure of projects that promised tax benefits led many to make investments that were unsound. When their real estate projects failed, as many did when the economy faltered in the middle of the 1970s, it was not just that they lost money on their investments. A tax calamity ensued as well.

---

[8] Tax laws try to prevent this from happening, but they do not always succeed. This was especially the case during this period.

A foreclosure is a recognition event for tax purposes. Hence, in the wake of foreclosure, not only have the doctors, dentists, and lawyers lost their investment, but they have to pay income tax on the difference between the amount at which the property is sold and the original value of the property less all the depreciation they had taken. In many cases, the property would have been completely depreciated, and they would owe taxes on the entire amount realized at the foreclosure. If they borrowed to acquire Blackacre, their tax liability could be much larger than the amount they invested in Blackacre in the first instance. To be sure, they enjoyed handsome deductions in the past, but that was cold comfort when they had spent that money or had it tied up in other, illiquid assets.

For this reason, the investors were eager to prevent a foreclosure sale. As long as they could do this, they could keep their investment intact and postpone the ultimate reckoning with the taxman. If they could use Chapter XII to prevent their lender from foreclosing, they could keep their equity position intact. They would not have a recognition event, and they would not have to take a significant tax hit. This possibility drove the dentists, doctors, and lawyers to have their real estate ventures file for Chapter XII.

Unlike Conrad Hilton, who wanted to retain ownership of hotels because of the special skills he brought to them, these investors were entirely passive. They wanted to remain owners not because of their management skills, but only because of the horrendous tax bill they would face if they no longer owned Blackacre. Such cases were not at all like restructuring a dry goods store. They did not involve small businesses with distant and dispersed creditors. Indeed, there was as a practical matter no business to reorganize. There might be an apartment building in which people lived, but these tenants would remain tenants regardless of whether the doctors, lawyers, and dentists owned the building or the bank did.

The language of bankruptcy – rehabilitating the debtor – was entirely out of step with what the investors in these tax shelters were doing. The courts that heard these Chapter XII cases invoked the language of the worthy debtor nevertheless. The case that epitomized this state of affairs was *In re Pine Gate Associates*.[9] Pine Gate was a set of

---

[9] 1976 U.S. Dist. LEXIS 17366; 2 Bankr. Ct. Dec. 1478 (N.D. Georgia 1976).

nondescript, newly built apartments in which too few wanted to live. The lender was owed $1.4 million. It had a nonrecourse mortgage on the property, so its recovery was limited to the value of the property.

When the lender tried to foreclose on Pine Gate, the investors began a Chapter XII proceeding. The filing of the petition stayed the foreclosure. At this point, the lender asked the judge to lift the stay, making all the familiar arguments that lenders make in such cases: the debtor was in default; management was poor; the property was worth far less than the debt. Because the debtor was not paying what it owed and was never going to pay back everything it owed, the lender argued that it should be able to foreclose. To prove its point, the lender brought in an expert who testified that the property was worth only $850,000.

The judge, however, refused to lift the stay. He believed the goal of debtor rehabilitation applied in such cases. Things were bad, but the judge did not believe that they were getting any worse. He allowed the debtor to propose a plan. At this point, the debtor came up with a plan that gave the lender $1.2 million in cash. It might seem that the lender would readily agree to such a plan. Its loan was nonrecourse. Its own expert had just testified that it would realize only $850,000 if the stay were lifted and the property were sold. Under the plan it was receiving half again as much in cash as it said it would receive if the judge had lifted the stay. How could the lender complain if the debtor was willing to give it more than its own expert had testified that the property was worth?

One suspects that the lender's expert had come up with a valuation focused too much on the task at hand – persuading the judge that the property was so deeply underwater that the stay should be lifted – rather than on the question of what the property was actually worth. The judge in *Pine Gate*, however, did not bind the lender to its earlier valuation. Rather than approve the debtor's plan outright, he gave the lender a chance to come back again with a different (and presumably higher) valuation.

But embedded in the logic of the judge's reasoning in *Pine Gate* was something that mattered much more than an artificially low valuation by an expert too anxious to please a client. Chapter XII gave the debtor, in addition to the ability to make a cash payment equal to the value of the property, the ability to give a new note equal to the value of the property.

If the debtor were entitled to pay the lender the judicially determined value of Pine Gate in cash, then the debtor could, under a parallel provision of the statute, reduce the amount owed the lender to the bankruptcy judge's valuation. The relevant language provided that the lender was entitled to the value of its debt. The value of that debt, if the loan was a nonrecourse loan, was necessarily going to be the value of the property.

In other words, through the magic of Chapter XII, the investors could emerge from the reorganization in exactly the same position, except that the debtor would owe its lender $1.2 million instead of $1.4 million. The lender would have neither cash nor the debtor's promise to pay what it had borrowed. It would have only the debtor's promise to pay a lesser amount.

Allowing debtors to propose such plans is troubling. Wiping out a creditor's interest while keeping those of junior stakeholders intact is exactly the mischief that led the court to strike down the foreclosure in *Howard*. The debtor is using a legal process only for the purpose of avoiding paying creditors what they are owed. No larger social goal is being vindicated in any of this. And Pine Gate was no railroad. There was no going-concern value. There was no collective action problem. There was no impediment to a market sale. Nor was Pine Gate a small business where an entrepreneur like Conrad Hilton could work magic if creditors agreed to scale back their claims.

In cases like *Pine Gate*, the language of debtor rehabilitation became unmoored from reality. The inability of the apartment complex to generate enough money to service the debt had nothing to do with whether people continued to live in the apartment building. A management company collected the rent and maintained the building. It (or another more or less similar management company) would oversee the building regardless of whether the dentists, doctors, and lawyers owned the building or the lender did. Allowing the lender to foreclose put nothing at risk and destroyed no value.

At the heart of the opinion in *Pine Gate* was the deeply flawed idea that scaling back or limiting the lender's claim and preserving the rights of real estate investors did something to rehabilitate the fortunes of the apartment complex. In the 1970s, many still accepted the idea that the value of a firm and its capital structure were necessarily linked. They implicitly believed that reducing the amount of a business's debt necessarily increased the value of the business. Today anyone who has a passing familiarity with modern finance knows this idea is wrong.

A business has value because of the cashflows it generates over time. The way the business's cashflows are divided among creditors and other stakeholders does not in the first instance affect the value of these cashflows. It is a basic axiom of modern finance that the division of cashflows does not itself affect the amount of cash that the firm makes. It remains constant whether it goes first to the lender or whether it is shared. Changing the way a pie is sliced does not change its size.

There might be particular reasons why a reduction in leverage might increase value, but it might reduce it as well. In the case of an apartment building, it most likely would, tax issues aside, have no effect whatsoever. But in the 1970s, this notion that it was hard to connect firm value with capital structure was foreign to judges.[10] They did not start with the idea that a debtor like Pine Gate was worth only the cashflows that its sole asset would generate over time. Giving any part of the cashflows to a junior investor was not possible if the debtor was worth less than what the senior creditor was owed and the senior creditor was entitled to be paid in full. For judges like the one in *Pine Gate*, trimming the lender's rights seemed to benefit junior investors without hurting senior ones. The judge could give a senior creditor a note equal to the value of the apartment building, and the debtor could have whatever was left.

This way of thinking, of course, was naïve. When a lender was owed more than the debtor's only asset is worth, it was not possible to give that lender a note equal to the value of the property and also allow the dentists, doctors, and lawyers to retain an interest in it. If the property was not worth enough to pay the lender in full, the lender must be

---

[10] Modigliani and Miller published their groundbreaking paper only in 1958. See Franco Modigliani & Merton Miller, The Cost of Capital, Corporation Finance and the Theory of Investment, 48 Am. Econ. Rev. 261 (1958). These ideas did not enter the legal academy until even later. The first paper to apply modern finance to secured credit was not published until 1979. See Thomas H. Jackson & Anthony T. Kronman, Secured Financing and Priorities Among Creditors, 88 Yale L.J. 1143 (1979).

undercompensated. A restructuring that left the limited partners with anything necessarily left the lender with too little.

Absolute priority required that senior parties were paid in full, and the rights of junior parties extinguished unless they contributed new value equal to the value of their stake in the reorganized entity.[11] But, as cases such as *Pine Gate* showed, the reality was something else. As a result, there was a tension between the rhetoric of the law and the way it played out in action. This disconnect invited hand-waving and sloppy thinking. Rather than give lip-service to absolute priority and do something else, it would have made much more sense to confront squarely the question of what sort of bargain advanced everyone's interests.

In the case of a leaky tax shelter, the dentists, doctors, and lawyers did put a higher value on a property like Pine Gate than anyone else. When they alone could enjoy tax benefits if they continued to own the property, there was a mutually beneficial deal to be made between them and the lender. The ambition of reorganization law, at least to the extent that preserving tax benefits was a value it should protect, should be to ensure there was a bargaining environment that allowed such a deal to be cut.

A similar but more compelling dynamic plays itself out in the context of a small business. Restaurants, building contractors, and service companies are often run by a single individual. The economic enterprise cannot be meaningfully separated from this entrepreneur. Take away the person who runs the restaurant, and there is nothing left other than a few tables and some used kitchen equipment. The construction company may have only a few pieces of heavy equipment subject to a security interest if the person behind it were to disappear. The accounting or consulting firm likely has no assets at all.

The creditors' rights are limited to whatever they can realize from liquidating the assets. The corporation is merely a vehicle that allows those who are self-employed to earn their livings as sole proprietors. The entrepreneur is in no sense tied to the firm. Someone who does

---

[11] *Los Angeles Lumber* contains dictum that suggests that new value must be in the form of hard assets, but this is not conceptually necessary. Indeed, the 2019 amendments to Chapter 11 allow old shareholders to remain in place by contributing sweat equity and human capital.

business in limited-liability form can walk away from it. There might be synergy between the entrepreneur and the assets, but the value that the two create together does not belong to the creditors. Without the entrepreneur, there is no going concern.

It is not a question of whether to favor creditors or the debtor. Instead, the aim of the law should be to create a mechanism that preserves the synergy, if any, that exists between the assets and the entrepreneur's human capital. The credit men believed that this goal was best achieved by entrusting them with the decision. Preserving viable firms was in their own self-interest. They needed to maintain their reputation as honest brokers who gave worthy debtors a second chance. More to the point, they wanted to ensure profitable customers remained in business. When they were able to act collectively, such as when they had a credit bureau ably staffed by someone like Henry Hirshberg, they could do this without legal intervention. When a bankruptcy reorganization was necessary, the decision should be entrusted to their collective judgment as they were better positioned to assess the debtor than a judge who sat apart from the day-to-day affairs of business.

There is something to be said for giving this sort of power to creditors as a group, but it is at least possible that in some environments the judge might stand in a better position to decide whether a business can rehabilitate itself successfully. Creditors might not be able to communicate with one another. They might not have a Henry Hirshberg to represent them. The stakes each one had in the business might be small. There might be bad blood between the debtor and one creditor, and that creditor's voice might prevent consensus from forming. At the same time, the judge might have seen enough small businesses to have formed good intuitions about which ones are likely to succeed.[12] In such an event, it is completely consistent with the principles of reorganization law to empower the judge to approve plans over the creditors' objection.

---

[12] Edward Morrison has shown that, as an empirical matter, judges are in fact adept at being able to distinguish between small firms that will succeed and those that will fail. See Edward R. Morrison, Bankruptcy Decision Making: An Empirical Study of Continuation Bias in Small-Business Bankruptcies, 50 J. L. & Econ. 381 (2007). At first approximation, judges do as well as a neutral and rational decisionmaker who possesses the same information.

Identifying the best decisionmaker is not easy and might change over time. The National Bankruptcy Conference, the group most responsible for the small business provisions of the Chandler Act, thought this power should rest in the hands of the creditors in the 1930s. The credit men believed they could make sensible collective judgments about a debtor's prospects. On the other hand, it was also the National Bankruptcy Conference that did the most to persuade Congress to shift the decision-making power to the judge in the case of small businesses in 2019. This new regime provides a streamlined procedure that allows the judge to approve plans that allow the self-employed to hold on to their small businesses without the consent of the creditors.[13]

Protecting worthy debtors is a deep-seated idea in reorganization law dating back to the time of the credit men, and it remains an essential part of the rhetoric that surrounds it. First principles, however, do not establish how one should go about discovering whether a debtor is worthy, whether the small business in question possesses value as a going concern or, to say the same thing, a happy synergy exists between its assets and the human capital of the entrepreneur who owns and runs it.

At the same time, it is important to understand that this kind of synergy is not implicated in the case of large reorganizations. Notions of the worthy debtor are out of place. All the managers are professionals. Indeed, by the time of the reorganization the managers themselves are often turn-around specialists.

Nor are the concerns about small individual investors that animated Frank and Douglas much in evidence in large reorganizations either. Virtually all the investors are sophisticated professionals. Whether junior or senior in the capital structure, the investor will be a hedge fund, a large pension fund, an insurance company, or a bank. By the time the reorganization starts, claims will have been transferred, often multiple times, and will rest in the hands of those who, far from wanting

---

[13] In particular, the total amount of debt must be below a specified threshold. In the United States, the businesses that fall under this threshold rarely have an identity apart from the owner. Even if it is healthy, such businesses typically close their doors when the owner retires. Even a fine-dining restaurant in a major city may be too large to qualify as a "small business" as the Bankruptcy Code defines it.

to avoid navigating the hazards of a corporate reorganization, relish doing battle there.

Mandating sharing for its own sake makes little sense when distressed debt investors inhabit every part of the capital structure. These professionals can adapt themselves to any priority regime. They will enjoy market returns on their capital. There is no fairness argument that requires either paying one investor before another or making sure everyone shares the hurt.

The choice of priority regime has no effect on firm value as long as the Modigliani and Miller assumptions hold.[14] Any benefit an investor gains from being made more senior ought to be exactly offset by losses borne by some other investor being made more junior. It is reasonable to start with the assumption that a firm with a capital structure built around relative priority will be worth the same as one built around absolute priority. In the American legal tradition, only one priority scheme emerged consensually, and it was the relative priority regime of the equity receivership.

Against this background, it makes sense to take a hard look at the challenges introduced by a regime such as absolute priority that requires a judicial valuation. Variations on *Pine Gate* show that respecting the right of a lender to be paid the full value of the asset that backs the debt is necessarily hard when there is a judicial valuation. Assume a case such as *Pine Gate*, but where the judge recognizes that the real estate lender is entitled to the full value of the debtor's only asset and makes valuations that are unbiased.

To ensure that absolute priority is respected, the court might require the dentists, doctors, and lawyers to contribute new value. If Pine Gate were worth $1.2 million, the judge could require an infusion of $100,000 on the part of the investors in the venture and give the lender a note worth $1.2 million. The real estate investors would still have a stake in the venture, and there would be no necessary short-changing of the lender's right to the full value of the property.

Similarly, the judge might allow real estate investors to stay in the picture if, notwithstanding a default and difficulties in the real estate

---

[14] See Eugene F. Fama, The Effects of a Firm's Investment and Financing Decisions on the Welfare of its Security Holders, 68 Am. Econ. Rev. 272, 272 (1978).

market, Pine Gate was worth more than the amount of the loan. Or there might be a more complicated capital structure, and the question would not be one of keeping the investors in place, but of allocating the rights between junior and senior creditors.

In these and other cases, however, everything turns on the judge's valuation. Even when the judge makes unbiased estimates of value, there will likely be departures from absolute priority. It might seem that the risk of undervaluation will be offset by the risk of overvaluation. As long as judicial valuations are unbiased, the senior creditor will do better when the property is overvalued and worse when it is undervalued, and it will balance out in the end. If the senior creditor is an institutional lender with a sufficiently large portfolio, it will receive the value of its collateral over the course of many cases. But things do not quite work out this way.

Assume that there is a junior and senior investor in a firm. The firm was once worth more than enough to pay the senior investor in full, but that is no longer the case. A senior investor is owed $100 and the firm is now worth only $100. Both the senior and junior investor have this information, but the judge does not. Assume the judge will make an unbiased valuation. Half the time, the judge will find that the firm is worth $125; the other half the time, the judge will find it worth $75.

If the judge finds that the firm is worth $75, the judge will simply give the entire firm to the senior lender. The judge undervalues the firm, but the junior creditor is not hurt. It would have received nothing even if the firm were accurately valued. But there is also a fifty-fifty chance the judge will find that the firm is worth $125. When this happens, the judge will award the junior creditor something even though the firm is not worth more than the senior creditor is owed. This benefit that the junior creditor enjoys when the judge overvalues the firm is not offset by any corresponding loss when the judge undervalues it. The senior creditor receives in expectation something less than $100.

Of course, senior creditors can anticipate such a shortfall and adjust the interest rate they charge accordingly, but to the extent that awarding one creditor priority over another has virtues (something that, of course, is not itself clear), these will be diluted to some extent because of valuation variance.

Valuation variance creates further problems when the debtor is allowed to contribute new value. Let us again assume that the firm is really worth $100 and the lender is owed $100. The judge is unbiased, but the judge's valuations exhibit variance. The judge will again find that the value is $125 half of the time and worth $75 the other half.

We have already seen that the old equityholders can capture value if the judge finds that the firm is worth more than it is. Consider what can happen when the judge undervalues the firm, and the debtor is allowed to contribute new value and can control the shape of the plan. When the judge undervalues the business, the judge will be willing to approve grants of stakes in the firm to those who contribute new capital at discounted prices. If the judge finds that the firm is worth $75, the old equityholders can propose a plan in which they contribute $25. The old equityholders take back 25 percent of the business, and the lender receives 75 percent.

The old equityholders have captured value because the equity for which they contributed new value was, like the firm itself, undervalued. The bankruptcy judge thinks that the firm with the new contribution of capital is worth only $100 ($75 plus $25) when in fact it is now worth $125 (the old firm's actual value of $100 plus the new capital contribution of $25). The old equityholders' one-quarter share of a firm worth $125 has a value of $31.25, even though they have put in only $25 of new capital.[15]

Another problem arises when the debtor is better informed about the true value of the firm than the judge, and the debtor is not committed to any particular course of conduct before finding out the judge's valuation. When the judge gives a value that is artificially low, the

---

[15] One must be a little careful here. There is another effect that goes in the other direction. It is possible to come up with some hypotheticals in which valuation uncertainty favors the senior investor. If the bankruptcy judge overvalues the property, the judge will, precisely because of the overvaluation, give the junior investors less than the judge thinks they are being given when the judge awards them a stake in the firm rather than cash. It is possible to come up with numbers where the judge's overvaluation more than offsets the benefit that the junior investor enjoys from valuation variance. See Bo Huang, Absolute Priority, Options, and Bargaining Dynamics in Chapter 11 Reorganizations (September 19, 2011) (unpublished manuscript), http://dx.doi.org/10.2139/ssrn.1930404.

debtor can cash out the lender. But when the judge gives a valuation that is artificially high, the debtor can just turn over Blackacre to the lender. The judge's valuation in expectation is again unbiased, but the debtor pockets value at the lender's expense when the valuation is low and is no worse off when the valuation is high.

We should not be shedding any tears for the lender. Lenders will take such possibilities into account when they make their loan. In expectation they will still enjoy a market return. But as long as there is noise associated with judicial valuations, and as long as the debtor has information the judge does not, these uncertainties will introduce complications, and reorganization professionals will have to devise ways to mitigate them.[16]

Of course, the magnitude of this problem turns both on how much noise is in the judge's valuation and on the amount of private information the other players have. It is possible that in cases like *Pine Gate*, the potential for this sort of strategic behavior is small. The dentists, doctors, and lawyers are not doing what they are doing in order to shortchange the banks. They are just trying to preserve the value of their tax benefits. It makes sense for them to remain owners of Pine Gate even if they have to pay the lender more than Pine Gate is worth. Nor are they exploiting private information. They are just dentists, doctors, and lawyers. They know no more about the value of Pine Gate than the judge.

Indeed, in a world of economically sophisticated bankruptcy judges doing unbiased valuations based on limited information, there is a risk of overcompensating lenders. In large measure because of *Pine Gate*, a number of provisions protect senior lenders from debtors that might otherwise take strategic advantage of the judge's inability to value the property perfectly. Still others offer senior creditors extra protection in single-asset cases. In this legal environment, senior lenders are no

---

[16] Senior lenders, for example, can offer options to junior stakeholders. These can substantially mitigate the problems of valuation variance. They are called Bernstein options after the lawyer who deployed them in his practice and provided a theoretical account. See Douglas G. Baird & Donald S. Bernstein, Absolute Priority, Valuation Uncertainty, and the Reorganization Bargain, 115 Yale L.J. 1930 (2006). Bernstein is the head of Davis Polk's reorganization practice and thus the heir to Francis Stetson, the lawyer who represented the Northern Pacific Railway in *Paton* and *Boyd*. Unlike Swaine, he understands the tight connection between options and priority rules.

longer exposed to the same risk of undervaluation they faced previously.

At the same time, however, little has been done to focus squarely on the difficulty associated with justifying a reorganization law in the context of simple real estate cases. The absence of a strong rationale matters because real estate cases are often invoked as precedents in large reorganizations. These are an awkward source of wisdom for large business reorganizations as they face radically different problems.

It might seem that the difficulties inherent in judicial valuations are a price worth paying in return for capturing the benefits of absolute priority. Alternative regimes might make it even easier for judges to play fast and loose with creditors' rights. If the investors must incur additional costs to protect themselves against these uncertainties, capital will be harder to raise. This is an objection commonly raised against the new European Directive that blesses what it calls "relative priority." Its version of relative priority is an altogether different beast from the relative priority regime of the equity receivership, however. In the American experience, relative priority was grounded on the idea that a reorganization was not a recognition event. Its foundations rest on bedrock principles of modern finance and can be defined rigorously, even if it is not as easy to articulate as absolute priority.

There is much to be said for a world in which a creditor's rights can be set out clearly. But absolute priority does little to distinguish itself over this dimension as long as it depends on judicial valuations. Relative priority as long understood in the United States, at least in a world in which option pricing is well understood, can also be set out clearly, and a firm can reorganize under it without there being a need for a judicial valuation.

Seen through this lens, the virtues of absolute priority over a regime of rigorously defined relative priority are not at all obvious. Assume that under a regime of absolute priority, a firm raises $95 from outside investors. It receives $49 from a senior lender in return for a promise to pay $50 in a year. At the same time, it receives $46 from a junior investor in return for a promise to pay $50 in a year. An efficiency explanation for absolute priority must show why the firm could not also obtain a total of $95 from senior and junior investors under a regime of relative priority in return for a promise to pay $100 in a year. Because of the higher risk, the senior investor, everything else equal, will not offer as much as $49 for the right to receive $50 in the future, but the junior investor faces correspondingly less risk and should be willing to offer more than $46.

Some justifications for absolute priority posit an agency problem.[17] The owner-manager of a firm seeks outside investment with the goal of maximizing the amount that can be raised. The outside investors have no easy way to tell whether the owner-manager is doing everything possible to make the venture succeed. Nor can they tell whether the owner-manager is taking unnecessary risks.

The owner-manager and the outside investors can minimize this agency problem by maximizing the share that the outside investors receive when things turn out badly. When owner-managers take nothing until and unless the investors are paid in full, they have every incentive to make the business succeed. They enjoy the benefit of each marginal dollar the firm makes and incur the cost of each marginal dollar the firm loses above the value of outside investments. In the presence of this or other similar agency costs, it makes sense to implement a regime of absolute priority.

Under this view, reducing agency costs is the main event. Departures from absolute priority have the effect of making outside investors less willing to lend in the first place and capital harder to secure. There might be competing considerations. For example, owner-managers might not be inclined to trigger a reorganization if they will be wiped out completely, and they may need to be given some incentive to remain with the firm. But departures from absolute priority undermine the need to ensure that the manager has the right incentives. They require justification. Absolute priority should remain the starting place.

This agency-cost rationale, however, fits poorly with modern debates about priority, at least as applied to large corporate enterprises. There is no agency problem between investors holding different layers of debt. None of them are charged with operating the firm. Investors in large, publicly traded firms entrust the operations of the business to professional managers.

---

[17] See Alan Schwartz, The Absolute Priority Rule and the Firm's Investment Policy, 72 Wash. U. L.Q. 1213, 1224 (1994).

It was once common to think that there was an agency problem in large corporate reorganizations because the managers were beholden to the shareholders. But in modern reorganizations, public shareholders hold little power. In the vast majority of cases, they are going to be wiped out. As soon as a firm is in financial distress, the managers pay more attention to the creditors who will control the firm going forward. By the time of the reorganization, the creditors hold many of the levers of power, and the managers know that these creditors will soon be the ones cutting their paychecks.

In short, when the priority debate is between sophisticated investors holding different layers of debt, one cannot use simple agency-cost theory to identify the optimal priority rule. There are, to be sure, other theories as to why some creditors strongly prefer absolute priority over relative priority.[18] Consistent with the structure of Anglo-American law, many of these theories are asset-based. A creditor might prefer to take a security interest in a particular asset because of that creditor's ability to monitor that asset's value and condition. A seller of a particular type of equipment might finance the sale and be able to ensure that the debtor properly maintains and insures the equipment. And if the firm is liquidated, the seller of the equipment might also be best equipped to repossess and sell it and realize its value. But asset-based priority justifications have a harder time explaining capital structures in which some creditors have blanket priority over all the assets of the firm.

There are, to be sure, some plausible justifications for blanket security interests over all of a firm's assets. For example, the optimal priority structure may depend upon which creditor is better positioned to monitor the debtor. A senior priority position might be more desirable for an investor who is distant and has a limited ability to detect misbehavior. An investor who is close to the debtor and able to monitor the debtor's business may find it worthwhile to bear the added risk that goes with low priority in return for a higher rate of return.

Alternatively, a creditor who puts in place a revolving credit facility might want priority over other investors. Such a creditor needs to be

---

[18] For a comprehensive discussion of the extent to which information imperfections can account for secured credit, see generally George G. Triantis, Secured Debt Under Conditions of Imperfect Information, 21 *J. Legal Stud.* 225 (1992).

close to the debtor and understand its business. More to the point, the loan is constantly in flux. The creditor must be confident that each new penny injected into the firm's operations can be recovered. Priority might make all the more sense if this creditor arrives late on the scene, and other sources of credit have disappeared. The existing debt that hangs over the business may shut off other sources of credit.

Investors as a group might be better off with the liquidity and the oversight such a senior lender provides. The senior investor with control rights may exercise them in a way that benefits the firm as a whole. This lender might, for example, insist on replacing the CEO long before junior investors and shareholders realize that the CEO needs to go. Alternatively, this lender might install a chief restructuring officer to sort out the financial condition of the firm and provide clear advice to all the stakeholders. Investors throughout the capital structure might benefit from the actions of the senior investor.

Of course, a senior investor's exercise of control is not necessarily value-enhancing for other investors. Senior investors are no Good Samaritans. They will focus on what advances their self-interest. Because senior investors enjoy first priority, they may play things too safe. They may decide, for example, not to allow their borrower to go forward with a risky product launch even though – from the perspective of the investors as a whole – it is likely to raise the value of the company. There are additional explanations for priority. For example, when one creditor has priority over another, neither wastes time or resources keeping a place in line.

But however sensible on their own, these explanations suffer from a recurrent problem. Each stands in tension with the other explanations. Both the presence and the absence of monitoring are used to explain why a creditor is senior or junior to another. The problem is not the lack of an explanation for absolute priority, but existence of so many.

Of course, the way investors structure their deals suggests that there must be some value in priority. In recent decades there has been a dramatic rise in second-lien financing. In these transactions, two creditors enter into a bargain with each other and with a common debtor in which one creditor takes a position junior to another. This creditor explicitly agrees to remain passive and allow the now-senior creditor to exercise control rights without interference. Sophisticated parties would not establish such priorities between themselves or parcel out control rights in this fashion, unless it was in their mutual interest. In addition, parties can (and do) enter into subordination agreements with one another, and these are enforceable in a corporate reorganization. The priority one enjoys over another must be doing something more than making one investor safer and the other less safe.

All such agreements, however, are written in the shadow of existing law. The way two parties allocate value between themselves when other investors enjoy absolute priority is not necessarily the same as it would be if all parties were subject to relative priority. Moreover, the priority rights bargained for today account for the constraints that current law places on the ability of junior creditors to waive their right to participate in a reorganization. For example, it is not clear that parties can change through agreement such things as the ability of junior creditors to object to asset sales. A senior lender might insist today on absolute priority only because other parts of the bargain are fixed.

Subordination agreements are in any event elaborately negotiated, and junior investors are rarely committed to refraining from asserting their rights unless and until senior creditors are paid in full. Indeed, subordinated parties sometimes bargain for the right to receive junior securities in a restructuring that give them part of the cashflows once the senior creditors receive as much as they lent originally. Such contingent rights, X-clauses as they are called, are examples of relative priority emerging through contract. Instead of being wiped out when the firm is not worth enough in expectation to pay the senior creditors in full, the junior creditors have what is in effect an option that is in the money when things go better than expected.

To be sure, private debt contracts do have a feature that suggests that parties bargain for absolute priority. Senior creditors almost always have an unqualified right to foreclose in the event of default, and debtors who file for a reorganization are usually in default. A right to foreclose is a right to insist on an immediate day of reckoning upon default, and this is exactly what absolute priority is. This might seem to suggest that parties regularly agree to enter a regime of absolute priority.

But it is a mistake to draw such an inference too quickly. A debtor can always put a stop to any foreclosure by filing for reorganization. Debtors cannot waive their right to reorganize. It does not matter what the agreement says. The lender does not have the ability to foreclose as a practical matter. This limits what we can infer from a contract that gives the lender a right to foreclose. When words in a contract have no legal effect, one cannot conclude that they reflect what is in the mutual interest of the parties. Bonds take the form they do because when they were first adopted for railroad reorganizations in the nineteenth century, they followed the form of real estate mortgages. Foreclosure rights may appear in bonds today not because they reflect a sensible allocation of rights, but because of path dependence.

The absolute priority rule can be captured and to some extent justified in rigorous economic terms. But this is not the way that those who brought the rule into being thought about it. Nor is it the way the judges received it. Because everything was subject to a judicial valuation, there was a great deal of play in the joints, and the strict priority system that absolute priority put in place in theory often gave way in practice. There are necessarily uncertainties inherent in applying absolute priority in a world that depends on a judicial valuation.

Reorganization law depends crucially upon the parties themselves finding common ground. In principle, as long as bargaining is sufficiently frictionless and parties are attuned to their own interests, undesirable liquidations should never happen. A deal is possible that makes some better off and no one worse off. This line of thought suggests that the virtues of a reorganization regime turn on whether it facilitates bargaining among the parties. The principal ambition of reorganization law – whether couched in the language of rehabilitation or not – is to make it possible for parties to negotiate with each other on something like equal terms. This has little to do with vindicating any particular priority scheme.

Designing a forum that leads to consensual deals is hard. It may not even be enough to focus on lowering the costs of bargaining. Consider the following hypothetical. There are four unsecured creditors, all of whom have claims of uncertain value. None brings any special value to the business, and each is focused only on maximizing what it receives in the reorganization. Let us assume that the firm is worth $14 and that any three of the four creditors can form a coalition in which they divide $12 among themselves and leave $2 for the excluded creditor.

No matter how frictionless the bargaining, there is no bargain that can be reached under these facts that is stable. In the language of game theory, the core is empty. The creditor who is left out of any given coalition can propose a deal that gives two members of the coalition more and still be better off than if cut out of the deal entirely and left with only $2. Reorganization law must be written in such a way as to make sure that such situations do not arise or at least not often. Of course, in this particular hypothetical, the empty core problem arises only because one creditor can be short-changed. This cannot happen when rights can be accurately valued, but this is the point. As Fischer Black memorably observed, "All estimates of value are noisy."[19]

In the end, what matters most is whether the rules of corporate reorganization – written or unwritten – allow parties to negotiate with each other once the reorganization begins. It should therefore come as no surprise that creating such a bargaining environment was what mattered most to those who gave decisive shape to modern reorganization law. They were the heirs of Paul King, and the next chapter turns to their story.

---

[19] Fischer Black, Noise, 41 J. Fin. 529, 533 (1986). For Black, a market was efficient if the price at which a security traded was somewhere between half and twice its true value.

7   BARGAINING AFTER THE FALL

By the middle of the 1970s, the deficiencies of Chapter X were too manifest to ignore. Those in control of a corporation in distress were reluctant to look to Chapter X to restructure debt as long as they had any other options. Because the absolute priority rule applied in Chapter X, insider shareholders were wiped out, something for which they had little enthusiasm and that led them to resist reorganization. Moreover, Chapter X mandated that an independent trustee be appointed to run the company. Hence, the managers who played a major role in initiating a Chapter X proceeding would lose their jobs the day they filed the case. Hence, they had little enthusiasm for Chapter X either. Very often, by the time a firm entered Chapter X, it was too late, and the only sensible course was to liquidate it and then only after significant delay and further loss.

Even when a firm that entered Chapter X might still survive as a going concern, the oversight that Frank and Douglas thought would prevent advantage-taking often prevented anyone from righting the ship. Trustees brought in to run large businesses were often industry executives with less than sterling track records. They were generally competent, but a large firm in trouble usually needed better. For smaller Chapter X cases, panel trustees were brought in. They were most often lawyers whose comparative advantage was liquidating a business, not running it.

The problems of many small businesses could be solved under Chapter XI, but Chapter XI was of little use when there was a secured creditor who proved recalcitrant, as Chapter XI provided no means for restructuring such debt. And when the businesses were large, there was another problem with Chapter XI. The SEC might try to convert it into a proceeding under Chapter X. Those in the small office at the SEC that handled Chapter X cases spent much of their energy arguing about whether a case filed under Chapter XI should be converted to one filed under Chapter X.

Reform of the law of corporate reorganizations attracted relatively little interest outside the reorganization bar. But the reorganization bar did care intensely about law reform. To be sure, as was the case with Paul King, restructuring lawyers had no interest in law reform that eliminated the niche they filled, but, apart from this, they cared a lot about making the law better. For them, negotiations were the lifeblood of reorganizations, and the aim of law reform should be to improve the environment in which these negotiations took place. They favored not the broad equitable principles that Douglas embraced, but rather narrower ones that focused the judge more squarely on getting the parties to reach a deal without worrying excessively about the substantive terms of the bargain they struck.

The ranks of bankruptcy professionals still included referees and lawyers who worked for the credit men. It also included lawyers whose practices focused on representing debtors in Chapter XI. These debtor lawyers embraced the idea of the worthy debtor in a way that was not merely aspirational as had been the case for lawyers of the credit men like Henry Hirshberg. These lawyers often had a belief in the ability of their debtors to make their businesses successful that was often more grounded in hope than experience. Like the judge in *Pine Gate*, these debtor lawyers were also less troubled by a process that did not respect the substantive rights of some of the players. They were willing to cast them aside if they thought doing so enabled a struggling firm to remain in business, often even when saving the firm did not make economic sense. That said, like the lawyers for the credit men, they were focused on making bargaining easier.

In 1970, Congress appointed a commission to review the bankruptcy laws and recommend reform.[1] Its reporter was Frank Kennedy. Like James McLaughlin, he was a law professor, a member of the

---

[1] Act of July 24, 1970, Pub. L. No. 91–354, 84 Stat. 468.

National Bankruptcy Conference, and a gentleman of the old school. The commission issued a report in 1973, and its proposals established the agenda of law reform for the rest of the decade. Many of those who served on the commission or who had helped it were members of the National Bankruptcy Conference, and the National Bankruptcy Conference generally supported the commission's proposals.

A major obstacle to reform, however, soon emerged. It stemmed from the role the commission envisioned for bankruptcy judges. There were two problems under the existing law that the commission identified. First, bankruptcy judges immersed themselves in cases in ways that were decidedly nonjudicial. Bankruptcy judges did more than simply police the bargaining. They were actively involved in the administration of the case and often of the business itself. At the same time, bankruptcy judges (as opposed to the district judges who also heard reorganization cases) possessed too little power. They had only a limited ability to resolve disputes. For the most part, when there was a dispute between the debtor and a third party, the bankruptcy judge could hear it only if the third party consented (or was deemed to consent). This limited the control they could exercise over the bargaining environment. It was hard to police the bargaining when the parties were free to take their dispute elsewhere.

The commission believed that in order to oversee the process effectively, judges had to step back from the active administration of the case. They should play no role in running the business. The stakeholders had to chart a course for the debtor themselves. At the same time, when disputes arose, there needed to be one-stop shopping. Bankruptcy judges should be able to resolve all the disputes between the players, not just those who gave their consent to the court's jurisdiction.

Changing the role of the judge in this fashion was not itself especially controversial, but to ensure that the bankruptcy judges would have the necessary power under the Constitution to resolve all the disputes that arose, the commission recommended that the bankruptcy judges no longer serve as adjuncts of the district court. Instead, they should serve as federal judges in their own right.[2]

---

[2] The ultimate compromise was to give judges expanded power without giving them life tenure. Achieving these two objectives consistent with the Constitution, however, has

This proposal to elevate the status of bankruptcy judges touched a raw nerve. Federal judges strongly opposed any bankruptcy reform that would make bankruptcy judges their peers. They believed bankruptcy judges were second-class citizens, and they wanted them to stay that way. Putting bankruptcy judges on a par with federal judges would double the ranks of the federal judiciary, and federal judges had little interest in diluting their own prestige. Chief Justice Warren Burger was especially averse to the idea of elevating the status of bankruptcy judges. He feared the prospect of bankruptcy judges wearing robes, using the judges' elevator, eating in the judges' dining room, and calling him by his first name.

For their part, bankruptcy judges were also opposed to this reform. They, of course, did not object in principle to having an enhanced status, but it was plain that many of them would not be reappointed if their status was elevated. Equally troubling was the possibility that bankruptcy reform would shortchange them on their retirement benefits.[3]

But unlike the chief justice, bankruptcy judges were not categorically opposed to bankruptcy reform. In response to the commission's bill, the bankruptcy judges came up with their own bill. They did it under the aegis of the National Conference of Bankruptcy Judges, a fraternal organization that, like the National Bankruptcy Conference, Paul King had founded many decades before.

The commission's proposal and the judges' bill, shaped by the National Conference of Bankruptcy Judges, were both put before Congress. Given the opposition of Chief Justice Burger, the leadership in Congress thought a bankruptcy bill could pass only if the bankruptcy bench and bar both strongly supported it. These legislators made it plain that, even if the chief justice's objections could be surmounted, bankruptcy reform could happen only if supporters of the commission's proposal and the bankruptcy judges reached consensus.[4]

proved elusive. See, e.g., Northern Pipeline Const. Co. v. Marathon Pipe Line Co., 458 U.S. 50 (1982); Stern v. Marshall, 564 U.S. 462 (2011).

[3] Compare H.R. 31, 94th Congress, 1st Sess. §2–103(g)(2) (1976) (Commission bill), with H.R. 32, 94th Congress, 2d Sess. §2–103(g)(2)(B) (1976) (judges' bill).

[4] Oral History of Ronald Trost, National Bankruptcy Archives, Randall J. Newsome Oral History Collection, 1993–1998, 2004, p. 18.

There was considerable common ground between the two proposals. Although the bankruptcy judges had many ideas, the only one to which they were firmly wedded was ensuring that bankruptcy reform would not take away their jobs or pensions. For their part, supporters of the commission's proposal had no strong ideological commitment to elevating the status of bankruptcy judges. They just wanted to ensure that bankruptcy judges had enough power to resolve the disputes that arose during a case. They had no problem if this could be done without making them the peers of other federal judges.

One young lawyer who was a particularly strong enthusiast for bankruptcy reform believed that a consensus could be forged if everyone was brought together at a single place and time. There they could iron out the differences between the commission's bill and the bankruptcy judges' bill. If everyone presented a united front, there was a decent chance that Congress would act. This lawyer promoted his idea at an annual meeting of the National Bankruptcy Conference. As often happens when a young and eager member of an organization makes a sensible proposal that requires considerable work, it was decided to charge this young lawyer with organizing the meeting. His name was J. Ronald Trost. One of the many gifted lawyers who had a hand in forging the 1978 Bankruptcy Code, Trost's approach to the reform of reorganization law epitomizes the dynamic at work during this era.

Trost was the archetypal bankruptcy professional who rose to prominence after the departure of elite Wall Street firms from the reorganization arena. Trost was born in Fresno, California, where his father was the credit manager at a clothing store. Its typical customer was a farmer in the Central Valley. Trost's family moved to Modesto and then to Sacramento, and he grew up there. As a teenager, Trost had a car, an active social life, and a desire to leave as soon as he could. At age seventeen, he went to Rice University and then to the University of Texas Law School, where he graduated near the top of his class in 1957. Trost spent time as a lawyer in the antitrust division of the Justice Department before trying to establish himself in private practice.[5]

---

[5] See David A. Skeel, Jr., Debt's Dominion: A History of Bankruptcy Law in America 134 (Princeton University Press 2001).

A young lawyer with Trost's stellar academic credentials and record in the Justice Department would ordinarily join a litigation group at an elite law firm, but Trost was Jewish. In the late 1950s, this excluded him from high-end law practice. Trost found a job at a small firm in San Francisco that enjoyed a less than stellar roster of clients. One of these clients was David Sweeney, a master fraudster doing time in San Quentin. Trost had to meet with the lawyers representing the trustee of Sweeney's now-bankrupt entities. These lawyers were trying to recover money on behalf of the victims of Sweeney's many defalcations, and Trost pushed hard for a settlement that favored his incarcerated client as much as circumstances permitted. Like everyone else who had to negotiate with Trost in subsequent decades, the reorganization lawyers were impressed. Once the case was wrapped up, they invited him to join their practice.[6]

When Trost started work at his new firm, he knew nothing about reorganization law, written or unwritten. Indeed, on his first day at the firm, Trost was asked to organize the sale of a piece of property free and clear of liens, and he had to ask what a lien was. Nevertheless, reorganization practice was ideal for him. Sorting through the complex problems of financially distressed debtors had always attracted the most gifted lawyers. Once the lawyers on Wall Street decided to follow their investment banking clients and dropped their reorganization practices, the best of those excluded from elite firms gravitated toward reorganization practice. It proved an arena where Trost could find worthy adversaries.

Trost was a quick study. Trost read *Colliers*, a multivolume bankruptcy treatise, from cover to cover. He analyzed every published opinion on bankruptcy law as it appeared. Trost soon established himself as an authority on bankruptcy, and he started his own firm, after having proved himself too independent and too contrarian for the reorganization lawyers who had first hired him.

Trost's strong views extended to reorganization law itself, and he pressed them in articles he wrote for law reviews and anywhere else he had the opportunity. It was just a few years later that he organized the

---

[6] Oral History of Ronald Trost, National Bankruptcy Archives, Randall J. Newsome Oral History Collection, 1993–1998, 2004, p. 7.

conference to find common ground between the bankruptcy judges and the supporters of the commission's proposal.

Trost's primary ambition for this meeting, which took place in Atlanta, was to forge a unanimous consensus that resolved all the outstanding differences, but Trost had no scruples against, to the extent that he could, steering the consensus towards his own vision of law reform. Under his cajoling, even the most die-hard acolytes of William O. Douglas gave ground.[7] Among the many issues that had to be settled, though at the time it did not seem especially important, was what to do with *Los Angeles Lumber*. It was here that Trost's views left an impression.

Trost believed reorganization law worked best on a playing field that had clear markers. Trost saw himself and his fellow Chapter XI lawyers as strong-willed gladiators who entered the arena, squared off with each other, and after a few blows and counterblows, struck a deal. The new reorganization law should create an environment that made such deal-making easier. It should provide a set of rules that laid out what parties could and could not do. It should demarcate the lines that could not be crossed and thereby establish a field of play. The exact substantive rights embodied in these rules were not as important as ensuring that the rules themselves facilitated negotiation. The judge was there to ensure the bargaining was done on a level playing field.

Trost did not favor any particular priority regime as a matter of first principle. Trost had no particular hostility to absolute priority, but he had no particular affinity for it either. He was relatively indifferent to high theory. What he wanted were priority rules – and reorganization rules more generally – that made bargaining easier. From this perspective, arming each individual creditor with a right to insist on absolute priority made little sense. It gave individual creditors the right to an expensive valuation hearing in front of a judge if the negotiations did not turn out exactly as they wished.

---

[7] Most notable of these was Vern Countryman, who was a Harvard professor, a former law clerk to Justice Douglas, and a fellow member of the National Bankruptcy Conference. See Testimony of J. Ronald Trost, Bankruptcy Act Revision: Hearings Before the Subcommittee on Civil and Constitutional Rights of the Committee on the Judiciary, House of Representatives, 94th Congress, 2d Sess., 1908 (1976).

Trost forged a consensus around a modified version of the absolute priority rule crafted to make negotiations easier. Those holding claims in a class could, as a group, insist on being paid in full before anyone junior to them received anything. This right did not erect a barrier to the participation of old equity in the reorganized firm. It just put the decision-making power in the hands of the creditors as a group. As Chapter XI had shown, the creditors as a group would be willing to waive this right when it made good business sense. But individual creditors like Thomas Case would no longer be able to disrupt an entire reorganization by demanding payment in full before anyone junior to them in the pecking order participated. Dissenting creditors could be bound to a plan that gave value to more junior classes if a supermajority of those in their class approved.[8]

Trost reflected the spirit of those who pressed for a new reorganization regime.[9] They wanted an environment in which it was easy for sophisticated professionals to chart a sound course for the business going forward. The managers of the old firm proposed a plan, and the senior creditors pushed back. Once they settled on a future for the business, the question was how to divide the pie. The senior creditors were willing to give ground because they wanted to resolve matters quickly and cheaply; the old managers were willing to give ground because, in the end, the senior creditors as a class had the right to freeze them out. It was in the interests of both to find a middle ground. *Los Angeles Lumber* was a mistake because it did not allow this.

---

[8] This position is reflected in a letter that the heads of the National Bankruptcy Conference and the National Conference of Bankruptcy Judges sent to Don Edwards, the chair of the subcommittee. See Letter from John Copenhaver, President, National Conference of Bankruptcy Judges, & Charles A. Horsky, Chairman, National Bankruptcy Conference, reprinted in Bankruptcy Act Revision: Hearings Before the Subcommittee on Civil and Constitutional Rights of the Committee on the Judiciary, House of Representatives, 94th Congress, 2d Sess., 1938, 1941 (1976). In its final form, the priority rule under the Bankruptcy Code also allowed "cramdown." As long as at least one class of creditors consented to a plan, even dissenting classes could be bound to it. The plan proponent needed, however, to show that claims in the class were being given stakes in the reorganized firm equal to the value of their old claim. Cramdown was not possible under Chapter XI.

[9] Among others, this view of reorganization law as creating a forum that facilitated fair bargaining was shared by the two congressional staffers responsible for drafting the Bankruptcy Reform Act of 1978. See Kenneth N. Klee & Richard Levin, Rethinking Chapter 11, 21 Norton J. Bankr. L. & Prac. 5 (2012).

The law of corporate reorganizations allowed for bargaining in which cooler heads would likely prevail, and as long as they did, economically viable firms would be able to reorganize successfully. Cashflows would be allocated as the dynamics of the bargaining dictated. To be sure, clients who had the good fortune to retain a forceful lawyer like Trost might do better than others, but the exact terms of the deal were not as important as ensuring that some deal was made. When the parties reached a deal, there would be no need for a judicial valuation. The judge could simply bless it as long as the bargaining process was untainted, and the plan met the formal requirements laid out in the statute.

For these reformers, whether a rule promotes bargaining was the critical question. Hence, they were naturally led to rules such as the one that required equal treatment for claims in the same class. It limited the extent to which those bargaining over plans could play one creditor off against another. A debtor could not promise better treatment for a creditor's claim under the plan in return for its support of the plan. Such rules prevented the simplest sorts of payoffs and bribes.

These reformers advanced more specific reforms with this general goal in mind. Trost, for example, believed that claims should be freely transferable. It was easier to do battle with people who chose to be in the arena than with those who had been dragged into it. Under the General Orders that were created to implement the Bankruptcy Act, the bankruptcy judge had to approve any transfer of a claim from a creditor to someone else.[10] Trost believed such rules needed to be changed, and eventually they were.[11]

Indeed, from Trost's perspective, if the requisite majorities of creditors reached a deal before the reorganization even began, so much the better. The debtor could present the plan to the judge at the outset, and all the judge had to do was review it. There was no need for a new round of negotiations and voting. The kind of tight supervision that Douglas

---

[10] For a discussion of these rules, see Chaim J. Fortgang & Thomas Moers Mayer, Trading Claims and Taking Control of Corporations in Chapter 11, 12 Cardozo L. Rev. 1, 20 (1990).

[11] The modern rule that took the bankruptcy judge out of claims trading emerged in the early 1990s.

envisioned for a reorganization was unnecessary. Trost persuaded his colleagues to add such a provision to the bill. Quite a number of modern reorganizations take advantage of this provision. Such "prepackaged" reorganizations last only a few weeks and sometimes even less. This is a distinct contrast to reorganizations under Chapter X, which might take a decade or more.

In pushing for the provision that made prepacks possible, Trost was not fashioning something out of whole cloth. Lawyers for the credit men had entered large Chapter XI reorganizations with preapproved plans. It is one example of the way Trost and the many other gifted lawyers put into the new law practices that first took root in Chapter XI.

Ronald Trost's particular contributions illustrate the understanding of the reorganization process that reorganization professionals of the era shared. They wanted the judges to use their oversight powers to ensure that the parties had space in which they could negotiate with each other. At the same time, these reformers were generally hostile to granting judges unbounded equitable powers of the sort that Frank and Douglas sometime seemed to embrace. The bankruptcy judge was to have no "roving commission to do equity."[12] The judge's job was to ensure bargaining that led to consensus and respected the rights of all the parties. The judge was to focus on ensuring that the bargaining process remained on track and was not distorted by bribes, side-deals, or ulterior motives.

Douglas believed that disclosure was a good thing in its own right. The reformers took a more nuanced view. They recognized that some disclosure was essential. Disclosure rules are a crucial feature of any forum in which bargains are made. At the medieval fair, goods for sale had to be on public display.[13] On the Chicago Board of Trade, traders must, under some circumstances, disclose their trading positions (though only to the exchange, not to their contracting opposites). All forums in which sophisticated parties meet and bargain have disclosure rules, and the one for reorganizations should not be the exception. But disclosure obligations bring costs with them. Hence, the judge should demand disclosure only of those things needed to ensure effective bargaining.

[12] United States v. Sutton, 786 F.2d 1305, 1308 (5th Cir. 1986).
[13] See Ellen Wedemeyer Moore, The Fairs of Medieval England: An Introductory Study 115 (Pontifical Institute of Mediaeval Studies 1985).

In the modern world of corporate reorganizations, many of the players are distressed debt investors who buy and sell their positions because they believe that they know more than others. The disclosure obligations that best facilitate arm's-length bargaining in such an environment are far from self-evident. Trade-offs are inevitable. Sellers will not answer every question their buyers put to them. And even the most sophisticated buyers will not insist that they do. Too many disclosure obligations discourage the players from gathering information in the first place.[14]

It might seem that those who bought their claims during the reorganization should at least be obliged to disclose the price at which they acquired their positions. But even this is not obvious. Those who acquire a claim in the reorganization receive the same distribution as those who have always held them. The face amount of the debt, rather than their purchase price, governs the payout. (Any other rule reduces the ability of holders of claims to transfer them.) How much they paid for their claims has no effect on their legal rights in the reorganization. Given this principle, disclosing the price at which they purchased their claims should not affect the terms of any bargain. If two investors hold the same asset, they should attempt to maximize its value, regardless of how much they paid for it.

One of the most sensitive pieces of information for traders is their reservation price, the amount at which they are indifferent between buying and selling. If a sophisticated trader in a commodity is willing to buy at twenty and is also willing to sell at twenty-two, it is a fair inference that the trader's research has revealed that the commodity is worth twenty-one. Requiring traders to disclose the price at which they are willing to buy and sell is tantamount to requiring them to disclose the information they have gathered. If they are forced to disclose such information, they have no reason to gather it in the first place. Disclosure of such information tends to make the market for claims less liquid. This likely impedes rather than facilitates bargaining.

But this is not to say that limiting disclosure obligations always facilitates bargaining. Cabining disclosure obligations makes the most

---

[14] See, e.g., Henry G. Manne, Insider Trading and the Stock Market (Free Press 1966).

sense when the underlying market is liquid. When the amount of trading that takes place in a given market is small, however, all bets are off. One can imagine environments in which multiple parties possess private information but none of them have an incentive to disclose what they know, even though each would be better off if everyone disclosed. Put differently, we face a collective action problem in which the individual benefits of disclosure are small, but the benefits of disclosure to the group as a whole are large.

Even if it is not easy to lay down with precision what disclosures the judge should require, it is possible to set out the basic parameters. The judge needs to focus on what is needed to resolve the matter in dispute and what information the parties need to be able to negotiate with each other. At the same time, judges have to be alert to the potential costs of disclosure, direct and indirect, even of things that seem irrelevant and innocuous. Achieving this balance and exercising discretion wisely are the heaviest burdens the bankruptcy judge must bear.

In contrast to those who preside over other judicial forums, judges overseeing a reorganization are often forced to decide questions when only some of the interested parties are before them. Sometimes only the moving party is in court. Policing effectively in such an environment requires drawing inferences from what is being said and who is saying it. In deciding whether to grant a motion, judges pay attention to those who are supporting the motion and to those who are opposing it.[15] Drawing such inferences requires knowing where the advocates are coming from, especially when only a limited number of them appear.

When an investor who holds a general claim against the estate also holds an even larger slice of the senior debt, that investor's willingness to bless a particular motion takes on a decidedly different cast. Hence, it may make sense to require those who appear in front of the judge to disclose their positions even if they do not have to disclose when or how much they paid to acquire them.[16]

---

[15] See Paul Milgrom & John Roberts, Relying on the Information of Interested Parties, 17 Rand J. Econ. 18, 19 (1986).

[16] Bankruptcy Rule 2019 requires certain disclosures from creditors serving on a committee other than the official creditors' committee, but the written law contains few other explicit disclosure obligations.

Judges may also need to mandate disclosure to make it possible for those trying to forge a plan to learn who owns what. It is hard to forge a consensual plan if parties do not know with whom they should be bargaining. The easier it is to identify the stakeholders, the more likely it is that a sensible plan of reorganization can emerge. The core idea here is a familiar one seen in many other environments. The better defined the property rights, the more valuable they are. Land becomes more valuable when its owner and its boundaries are easy to identify from public records.[17] Quite apart from whether someone wants to buy or sell land, landowners can use their land more effectively if it is easy for them to learn who their neighbors are. Similarly, negotiating in a reorganization is easier when those trying to bargain know who needs to be given a seat at the table.

Disclosure, of course, does not itself end the matter. Even if judges know what they need to police the parties effectively, actually policing the parties is the main event. It is hard to set out comprehensively the rules needed to facilitate effective bargaining. The substantive rules, such as the modified version of the absolute priority rule that Trost promoted, only set out the field of play and the basic rules of the game. To be an effective referee, the bankruptcy judge must be a master of the unwritten rules. Referees cannot hand out so many yellow cards that they disrupt the flow of the game, but referees who hand out too few lose control. There is no written rule that suggests that a player's misdeeds accumulate, but everyone understands that they do. A single hard tackle might not merit a yellow card, but a second, identical one by the same player will. A practice that is beneficial in some cases can do mischief in others.

At the same time, the bankruptcy judge must ensure that the basic rules of the game are followed, quite apart from the substantive merits of the rules themselves. Consider the following hypothetical. The debtor owes a supplier $120 and its other creditors $240.[18] Assume

---

[17] Gary D. Libecap & Dean Lueck, The Demarcation of Land and the Role of Coordinating Property Institutions, 119 J. Pol. Econ. 426 (2011).

[18] This hypothetical and the related ones that follow are loosely based on the facts of Czyzewski v. Jevic Holding Corp., 137 S. Ct. 973 (2017). For a comprehensive view of the case and structured dismissals, see Bruce Grohsgal, How Absolute is the Absolute Priority Rule in Bankruptcy? The Case for Structured Dismissals, 8 William & Mary Bus. L. Rev. 439 (2017).

that these other creditors control the creditors' committee, and that the creditors' committee is in control of the case.

The supplier has an independent action against a third party that has no relationship of any kind with the debtor. This action, if brought, will net the supplier $80 with certainty. The supplier, however, does not have the resources it needs to bring the action unless it receives a distribution from the estate.

Assume that the third party approaches the creditors' committee and offers to contribute additional money to the estate on the condition that neither this money nor any other estate assets are distributed to the supplier. Accepting this offer makes the estate better off. It increases the total amount that is distributed to the creditors. Maximizing the value of the estate is an oft-trumpeted ambition of the law. Nevertheless, the judge will not allow such a deal to go forward.

Allowing those who control the reorganization process to compromise reorganization's pro-rata sharing rule for a price invites mischief. Allowing those with their hands on the levers of control of the case to sell the process invites them to spend resources looking for such opportunities. This anti-hijacking principle has nothing to do with the particulars of the pro rata sharing rule. It would apply equally to any other rule governing the distribution of assets of the estate. Following the distributional rules, whatever they are, is essential to an orderly process.

Once the rules of the game are in place and the game begins, a player should not be able to change the rules unilaterally. This anti-hijacking principle is not set out explicitly in the statute nor in Supreme Court precedent, but there is little doubt that this idea is embedded in the modern understanding of the principles that originated with the Statute of 13 Elizabeth.

In asserting their rights to the assets of the estate, investors are free to choose the course that maximizes the value of their own stake in the firm. But parties cannot make side payments with a view to tilting the bankruptcy process in their favor. Participants in the bargaining cannot use their position to act opportunistically to further their outside interests. A third party who buys claims in order to exercise control in a way that promotes the interests of a competitor, for example, will likely find its debt equitably subordinated. It will have to wait until other creditors at the same priority level recover before it receives anything.[19] A creditor who serves on the creditors' committee cannot dissuade others from purchasing claims in order to secure them at a lower price for itself.[20]

Applying these ideas, of course, is not always easy. Someone involved in negotiating a plan may make a transfer to another player during the course of bargaining. Actions like this are occasionally needed to buy peace from junior parties. In a perfect reorganization regime, junior parties should not be able to invoke procedures that are unnecessary, but it is likely impossible to create rules that completely prevent junior creditors from triggering wasteful litigation. As a result, a junior creditor may have the right to bring a procedural objection that adds little or no value to the estate as a whole. A senior creditor is not distorting the process if it makes a payment to keep such an objection from being raised.

When a senior creditor who manifestly is owed more than the firm is worth wants to bring the reorganization process to a speedy conclusion, the senior creditor's decision to pay money to someone to truncate unnecessary procedures is, in the view of many judges, entirely appropriate and falls within the domain of ordinary bargaining behavior, provided it is fully disclosed. In their view senior creditors should be able, with appropriate disclosure, to make payments to junior creditors and to professionals who have done work for the debtor, the creditors' committee, and other constituents to ease frictions, at least when the amount of money is modest in the grand scheme of things.

It is not surprising that many judges do not find it troubling when the senior creditor agrees to pay for the professionals who have done work for others. The process is being run for the benefit of the senior creditor when it is owed more than the business is worth, so it is entirely sensible that the senior creditor pays the toll. The senior creditor should be able to use what is, in effect, its own money to bring the case to

---

[19] See LightSquared LP v. SPSO LLP., 511 B.R. 253 (Bankr. S.D.N.Y. 2014).

[20] Indeed, such a creditor risks far more than having its claim subordinated. For an example of a creditor who found himself subject to criminal prosecution for engaging in such behavior, see Gregory Zuckerman & Soma Biswas, Hedge-Fund Manager Who 'Came Undone' Is Headed to Prison: Dan Kamensky broke bankruptcy laws with a series of frantic messages over a few hours in a long-running fight over Neiman Marcus, Wall St. J. (June 12, 2021).

a swift conclusion when the relevant issues are plain for all to see. Such payments are analogous to those routinely made when civil litigation is settled. Judges have little difficulty, however, striking down transfer payments that are too large or otherwise suspect.

When a class objects to the confirmation of a plan that gives value to out-of-the-money junior stakeholders, judges can invoke the statutory mandate that a plan be "fair and equitable." A plan cannot skip over an intervening, nonconsenting class. This "anti-gifting principle" operates even when there is strong evidence that the senior creditor is owed more than the firm is worth. It ensures that the plan formation process is squeaky clean.[21] The "fair and equitable" requirement for plan confirmation, however, is only one manifestation of the largely unwritten regulatory apparatus that governs bargaining in a reorganization. The judge must distinguish innocuous "tips" from forbidden "gifts" across a variety of domains. The judge must ensure that the bargaining remains focused squarely on maximizing the value of the debtor's estate, and not on the value of outside interests. This idea is a general one and applies even if the statutory "fair and equitable" mandate is not in play.

Consider a variation on the hypothetical discussed earlier. The supplier and the other creditors are again owed $120 and $240 respectively, but the debtor's sole asset is a lawsuit against a third party that is costless to bring and will yield $120 with fifty-fifty probability. In addition, the supplier has a standalone cause of action unrelated to its dealings with the debtor. If the supplier can find the resources to bring the action, it will succeed with certainty and receive a judgment for $80. The supplier, however, can bring this standalone action against the stranger only if it receives a large enough distribution from the debtor's reorganization.

The supplier does not have the right incentives with respect to the debtor's settlement of the suit with the third party. The supplier may press for settlement on the cheap if its share of the settlement gives it enough to pursue its own piece of litigation. On the other hand, the

[21] The Second Circuit put it this way: "[I]f the parties here were less scrupulous or the bankruptcy court less vigilant, a weakened absolute priority rule could allow for serious mischief between senior creditors and existing shareholders." See DISH Network v. DBSD North America, Inc., 634 F.3d 79, 100 (2d Cir. 2011).

supplier might fight against a settlement that is in the interests of the creditors as a group if the settlement did not bring enough to finance the supplier's own litigation. In the extreme case, the supplier might urge the debtor to refuse all settlements and try to hit a home run.

Under these facts, those negotiating on behalf of the debtor should not approve any settlement for less than $60. For the same reason, they should approve any settlement for more than $60 (50 percent of $120). A settlement for less than $60, though less than the expected value of its claim, might still be enough to enable the supplier to bring its own action. It is possible that the aggregate wealth of all of the creditors as a group is maximized if the supplier gains the resources to bring its action against the stranger. But this is irrelevant. This benefit to the supplier is not a benefit *to the estate*. The supplier's cause of action is separate from its rights against the debtor and cannot form any part of the settlement calculus.

Consider another variation, one that introduces side payments. The only asset of the estate is again a lawsuit against a third party and the creditors' committee is again leading the negotiations. The expected value of the lawsuit, however, is small, and it is doubtful that the resources can be found to bring the lawsuit or that any lawyer will take it on a contingent fee basis. The best the creditors' committee can do is to dig a little deeper. The third party offers to settle the action. As part of the settlement, the third party also agrees to pay out of its own pocket the fees and expenses of each member of the creditors' committee.[22]

The third party's offer to pay the fees should give the judge pause even in the absence of any evidence that the settlement is unreasonable. The third party might have any number of reasons for settling early and keeping the creditors' committee from doing additional digging. For example, there might be a bad email that would make prosecution of the case against the third party easy.[23] In order to ensure such an email

---

[22] The Bankruptcy Code provides for payment of the expenses of the committee as an administrative expense that is paid first, but the expenses of the individual committee members are not cognizable claims at all. Each creditor must bear them.

[23] For an example of a case in which an email satisfied a key element of a cause of action, see In re TOUSA, Inc., 422 B.R. 783, 794 (Bankr. S.D. Fla. 2009).

never comes to light, the third party might be willing to pay something to the committee and its professionals.

The members of the committee might be better off taking the side payment rather than pursuing the litigation. Each dollar of the side payment is an extra dollar they can keep, but any value they capture for the estate by litigating the claim has to be shared. They are willing to take a smaller payment for themselves in order to settle, even when the expected benefit of the creditors as a group is larger if they continue to pursue the litigation.

Because the creditors' committee must focus on the interests of the creditors as a group, it is important to ask whether any particular settlement has the effect of disturbing the committee's focus, which should be on advancing the rights of all the stakeholders. Incentives can be distorted with side payments, such as offers to pay expenses, but they can be distorted in many other ways as well. Indeed, whenever value passes from one player in the reorganization process to another, such a distortion is possible, and the judge is empowered to scrutinize such transactions and ask hard questions.

Imagine that a debtor has a senior lender, substantial priority tax claims, and a pool of general creditors. The debtor plans to auction the company.[24] It soon appears that the senior creditor plans to credit-bid. Unless the creditors' committee works hard to discover a flaw in the senior creditor's lien or find some other buyer, the senior creditor's credit bid will be unchallenged. Negotiations over auction procedures ensue. In return for an agreed-upon sales process, the senior creditor agrees to pay the professionals of the committee and provide several million dollars to the creditors' committee for distribution to the general creditors. When the senior creditor proves to be the high bidder, the priority tax claims are left unpaid, and the general creditors end up with something.

These payments might be side payments that distort the process. The payment to the creditors' committee may have had the effect of short-circuiting the due diligence that a well-run reorganization sale process requires. Of course, the payment to the creditors' committee

[24] See In re ICL Holding Co., Inc., 802 F.3d 547 (3d Cir. 2015).

did not prevent the tax collector from challenging the liens or finding other buyers, but not all parties are equally well positioned to take an active role in the case. The government's tax lawyers are not privy to the particulars of the business and lack expertise in corporate reorganizations. By contrast, the creditors' committee has access to information about the debtor and the debtor's business, and its professionals are used to the reorganization playing field. The committee is much better able to assess whether the senior creditor's proposed auction would yield top dollar. The side payment might have induced it to look the other way.

On the other hand, all that may be at work is a tip. The senior creditor was not trying to prevent an auction that secured top dollar, but rather was striking a bargain that avoided unnecessary and costly procedures. The trick is distinguishing between illegitimate side payments that pay someone to look the other way and legitimate tips that avoid unnecessary process. Because the payment is coming from the pocket of the senior creditor, property of the estate and its equal division are not implicated.

When the question is one of policing the behavior of creditors during the reorganization process, the judge is not asking whether some creditors received more from the estate than they should. The problems facing the judge arise regardless of whether a distribution is involved or not. Instead, the judge is asking whether the overall negotiations were conducted in a fashion that can be trusted to maximize the value of the assets in the reorganization forum. Protecting the bargaining environment rather than ensuring proper division of the assets is the task at hand.

Many other variations are possible. Consider a case in which a substantial shareholder of a business is also its CEO. The debtor proposes a plan in which the equity of the reorganized firm will go entirely to the old senior creditor. The senior creditor agrees to keep the CEO on as a consultant after the reorganization. The general creditors receive nothing under the plan and oppose it. The debtor puts on expert witnesses to show that the business is not worth enough to pay the senior creditor in full.

The judge must decide whether to uphold the general creditors' objection to this plan. It is possible that the CEO might be taking a payment in return for tacitly agreeing not to unsettle the senior creditor's plans. The consulting contract is a side payment from the senior creditor to the CEO. The lure of a hefty fee for little work makes the CEO less inclined to reveal information that shows the firm is worth enough to put the general creditors in the money.

Alternatively, the reasons for the bargain with the CEO may be altogether benign. The CEO may be agreeing to provide future services in an arm's-length transaction. If the firm is not worth enough to pay the senior creditor in full, then the firm belongs to that creditor. Such a senior creditor is entitled to credit-bid for the firm and retain whomever it wants as a consultant. If the judge finds that the transaction is offered to the CEO as a provider of future services, the bankruptcy judge should not strike it down. Such services are not assets of the estate.

The bankruptcy judge's ability to ensure the integrity of the reorganization process extends beyond transfers from one stakeholder to another. Assume, for example, that the CEO is not a shareholder at all. The senior creditor offers a lucrative consulting contract even though it is clear that the services are not needed. (The CEO has, for example, retired and moved out of state.) The bankruptcy judge can refuse to confirm such a plan on the ground that it was not proposed in good faith.[25] What matters is whether the side payment is being made because of the control the CEO exercises over the process, not whether the CEO is a stakeholder or is receiving property of the estate. The unwritten principles at work apply equally whether a plan is being confirmed, a going-concern sale is to be conducted, or a dispute is being settled.

Whenever side payments become large enough, the judge is likely to find that what are characterized as "tips" are nothing of the sort. They are just the price that the senior creditor is willing to pay to insulate its plan from close scrutiny. The judge must ensure that parties who exercise control work to maximize the value of the estate. As we saw in *Young v. Higbee*, stakeholders cannot strike deals in which they agree to drop objections in return for payoffs that go only to them.

---

[25] Bankruptcy Code §1129(a)(3). For a variation on these facts, see In re Bush Industries, Inc., 315 B.R. 292 (Bankr. W.D.N.Y. 2004).

The ability of parties to divert value is limited only by their own imaginations. It is not even necessary for money to change hands. A plan might include a rights offering that gives one of the players the ability to acquire an interest in the reorganized entity at a discounted price.[26] The discount might reflect what is necessary to obtain the commitment of new capital that the business requires, but there is a less innocent possibility. It might be the price paid to persuade someone with influence to look the other way.

Value can also be diverted through a "backstop." A backstop gives creditors the ability to take cash instead of a stake in the reorganized venture. There are good reasons for having them. A plan proponent might want to give a note in the reorganized firm to those in the most senior class and provide for the new equity to go to a more junior class. The plan proponent needs to show that the senior class is being paid in full, but it may be hard for the investors to know whether the new securities are worth what the plan proponent claims.

The plan proponent can allay this concern by obtaining a backstop. The provider of the backstop promises to buy the new securities at the value set out in the plan in the event that the old creditor would rather have cash instead. The willingness of a third party to buy the securities at a particular price provides evidence of their value.

But a commitment to buy securities for a fixed price does not magically appear. The plan proponent must pay the person who is furnishing the backstop. When the person who provides the backstop is also a player in the reorganization process, there is again cause for concern. The fee for the backstop might reflect the fair market value of the backstop, but the price might also be much more than the market price. When this is the case, the fee taken for the backstop constitutes a side payment in substance though not in form.

Sensibly distinguishing between backstops that are legitimate from those that divert value requires judgment and the sound exercise of discretion. It is a problem cut from the same cloth as the prohibition against "gifting" embedded in the fair and equitable test. These and other devices can arise in many contexts, and again the principles long

---

[26] For an excellent discussion of rights offerings and backstops, see Jane Lee Vris & Alexandra S. Kelly, Rights Offerings Get Popular and Contentious, N.Y. L. J., March 7, 2011.

immanent in the law of corporate reorganizations empower the judge to deal with them.

Nothing in the written law sets out how the judge should go about distinguishing between legitimate uses of devices such as rights offerings and backstops. It may not be possible to write such a rule. Instead, judges must rely on their inherent power to demand the information they need to understand the dynamics behind the proposals that are put before them. The judge must exercise the power, derived from the Statute of 13 Elizabeth and reshaped by those who crafted the modern law, to oversee the reorganization process.

The approach any particular judge takes varies. There is little doubt however that a judge who thinks a rights offering is a payoff in disguise can tell the parties in court or in chambers that no plan will be confirmed if it contains such a rights offering.[27] The parties must continue to negotiate and figure out how to confirm a plan without it. That the judge can cite no authority for this refusal is irrelevant. A judge's refusal to confirm a plan is not appealable.[28]

The oversight that the judge is exercising in this context is more stringent than the oversight that Victor Morawetz thought appropriate. For him, the judge was to intervene only when there was affirmative bad faith. This posture towards bargaining is not appropriate. As the Supreme Court put it long ago, a court should not "become the mere silent registrar of the agreements."[29] At the same time, the judge should stop short of the oversight that Frank and Douglas advocated. The judge is not there to ensure that the bargain the parties reach gives everyone a fair deal. There are no widows or orphans here. The judge merely ensures that the bargaining between sophisticated parties takes place on something like equal terms.

Setting out exactly what the judge must do is far from easy and hard to capture in statutory text. Outright prohibitions – such as a ban on transfers of value from the debtor to prepetition creditors other than their pro rata distributions from the estate – cut too broadly. Judges need to be able to approve transfers of estate assets to prepetition

---

[27] At least one retired bankruptcy judge who routinely heard major cases took this view.

[28] Bullard v. Blue Hills Bank, 575 U.S. 496 (2015).

[29] Louisville Trust Co. v. Louisville, New Albany & Chicago Railway, 174 U.S. 674, 688 (1899).

creditors when such transfers leave the estate better off.[30] There are problems of proof in many cases, but clear examples of value-enhancing transactions are easy to find.

Consider frequent flyer miles in an airline reorganization. The obligation of an airline to provide additional services (in the form of free travel and upgrades) generates a "claim" within the meaning of the Bankruptcy Code. Because the obligation arose before the filing of the petition, it is again a prepetition claim that ordinarily would be cashed out at cents on the dollar just like any other. But few doubt that the judge can approve a motion to honor frequent flyer miles. In many instances common sense must prevail. Treating such obligations as prepetition claims to be cashed out at pennies on the dollar is bad business. All the other creditors are better off if these obligations are fully respected.

The relevant question then is not whether some creditors receive more than others, but rather again whether what the debtor wants – the continued business of frequent flyers – is something that already belongs to it. As the frequent flyers have no obligation to continue to fly with the debtor, the estate needs to keep them happy. That the frequent flyers happen to be prepetition creditors is neither here nor there. As long as the estate has no claim on their future patronage and is better off spending money to secure it, it needs to be able to cut a deal with them.

When a payment to a prepetition creditor is proposed and someone objects, the judge, in addition to assessing the evidence that it is value-enhancing, will focus as much on the process that led to the proposal. From the judge's perspective, the question is whether the process itself was one that allows the judge to infer that the deal being presented is a good one and alternatives are not available.

The example of frequent flyer miles involved payments to entirely passive prepetition creditors. Passivity on the part of the beneficiaries

---

[30] This power is again the province of unwritten law. There are few appellate opinions to support the idea that judges have this power, even when it comes to something as sensible as paying workers the wages they are owed for work done prepetition. The case usually cited to show that bankruptcy judges have this power is In re Kmart Corp., 359 F.3d 866 (7th Cir. 2004). This case, however, actually struck down such a payment, although in the course of doing so the court did suggest that such payments might be permissible if they maximize the value of the estate.

of the transfer made it easier for the bankruptcy judge to conclude that those controlling the estate are paying them because it is good business. Side payments do nothing to grease the skids if those receiving them are not exercising any control over the business. But this is not always the case. Consider *Chrysler*.[31]

When Chrysler filed for Chapter 11, it proposed selling its assets for $2 billion, far less than Chrysler's senior creditors were owed. But if no one (including the senior creditors) valued these assets more than this amount, then such a sale was the course that would bring the greatest benefit to the creditors as a group and should be welcomed.[32] The buyer, however, also proposed giving several billion dollars to prepetition general creditors. (These creditors were retirees who were owed health benefits.)

The judge needed to decide whether the additional payment by the buyer to prepetition creditors was objectionable. The focus in the first instance should have been on why the buyer wanted to make the payment to the retirees. The buyer – in effect, the federal government – may have simply wanted to bestow largess upon them. In this event, the payment was not problematic. A third party's desire to bestow largess on a prepetition creditor does not interfere with the reorganization bargain. Indeed, in the absence of any other buyer willing to pay anything close to $2 billion, Chrysler's senior creditors were themselves beneficiaries of government largess. As such, they were hardly in a position to complain that someone else was receiving largess as well.

More likely, however, the buyer chose to pay the benefits to the retirees because the existing workers would have gone on strike if the buyer had left the retirees high and dry. Reorganization law puts in place rules like the automatic stay that constrain the efforts of prepetition creditors to take actions against the debtor to extract the payment of prepetition claims. Ensuring that there are procedural rules that prevent such hold-up behavior is part of maximizing the value of the

---

[31] In re Chrysler LLC, 576 F.3d 108 (2d Cir.), vacated, 558 U.S. 1087 (2009).

[32] This discussion elides another difficulty in the case. The bankruptcy judge may have approved procedures that chilled other bidders. The auction process was set up in such a way as to make it hard to submit liquidating bids. This was a mistake. Senior creditors should always be able to object to a process in which the debtor's assets are being sold for less than their true value.

estate. But such tools do not always work. And in this case, they would not.

Unequivocal mandates of federal law – in this case, the Norris-LaGuardia Act – prevent the judge from ordering the workers back to their jobs, even if the workers' intention is only to force the debtor to honor a prepetition obligation. If their collective bargaining agreement has expired, workers can refuse to do their jobs for any reason or no reason at all.[33] The judge lacks the authority to order them back to work, and in the absence of such authority, the implicit threat of the workers in *Chrysler* to strike if the retirees were not paid was credible.

One could imagine a reorganization regime that prohibits all payments to prepetition creditors. If the judge lacks the power to give in to a threat, the threat might not be made in the first place. If the strike could do the workers no good, they might not choose to strike in the first place. The ban might work in the same fashion as a law that prohibits the payment of ransom. When the judge's hands are tied, the incentive to make a threat in the first place disappears.

But such outright prohibitions cut broadly. They might lead to desertion by the frequent flyers and many others whose goodwill is essential to the debtor's business. They will stop doing business with the debtor if the debtor breaks faith with them, regardless of whether the debtor's hands are tied or not.

If the estate has no right to insist that frequent flyers or workers continue to do business with the debtor, it may need to pay them money to keep them happy. In such a case, the estate is using its resources to acquire something to which it otherwise has no legal right. There is nothing inherently problematic about such transfers to the extent that they enhance the value of the estate. Reorganization policy is implicated only if the frequent flyers or workers are undermining the collective proceeding and the judge has an ability to do something about it.

Another type of transaction with prepetition creditors who have negotiating power arises when the debtor seeks postpetition financing. Before the petition is filed, the debtor often has a relationship

[33] In a decision that is hard to defend, the Second Circuit has, however, found an exception when the collective bargaining agreement involves the Railway Labor Act. See Northwest Airlines Corp. v. Association of Flight Attendants-CWA, 483 F.3d 160 (2d Cir. 2007).

with a bank to provide it with credit. At the time of filing the debtor typically owes that bank a sizable amount under its existing credit facilities, and the bank is fully secured. To keep doing business as usual, the debtor needs new credit to fund its operations. The bank that provided the financing prepetition is willing to provide postpetition financing, but only on the condition that a portion of the new loan be used to pay off the debtor's old loans from the bank.

The effect of such a "roll-up" is to pay off the postpetition financer's prepetition debt. The bank ceases to be a prepetition creditor and instead becomes an extender of postpetition credit and enjoys the stronger rights associated with that status. Roll-ups, by their nature, lead to prepetition debt being paid off, and paid off with first priority.

The benefit the bank enjoys from a roll-up might be small. Its debt is fully secured, and it is entitled to be paid first anyway. The effect of the roll-up might be not so much to ensure payment as to give the bank more control of the reorganization process.[34] But whether small or not, the bank is exploiting its leverage.

Sometimes judges must prove they will walk away from what appear to be value-maximizing transactions in order to deter strategic behavior. A judge who gives in to destructive strategic behavior invites such behavior in future cases. The judge must also take account of the difficulties in determining whether the transaction is in fact aboveboard and wealth-enhancing. Payments to insiders and strategic players are always troublesome. The more ties the estate has with a party, the more likely it is that the deal is not what it appears to be. And the more exotic the transaction, the less likely it is that the bankruptcy judge can completely understand what is going on.

A judge's refusal to bless a transaction is not the end of the matter either. If a transaction that the judge refuses to approve would leave the remaining creditors better off, there is still a deal to be struck. If all the

---

[34] If prepetition debt is rolled up so that all of the debt is postpetition, the debtor loses the ability to cram down a plan over the bank's objection, as, in the absence of a waiver, postpetition expenses have to be paid in cash at the time of plan confirmation. Bankruptcy Code §1129(a)(9)(A). In other words, a roll-up gives the bank the right to cash equal to the amount of its claim instead of a right to insist on a note that the bankruptcy judge finds is equal to the value of its claim.

affected parties consent, no reorganization policy prevents such a deal from being consummated. For this reason, a judge's inability to prevent a party from making a credible threat and the judge's refusal to approve a transaction with a third party will not necessarily leave the prepetition creditors without the benefit of a mutually beneficial bargain.

The law of corporate reorganizations posits the existence of a collective action problem that prevents the parties from reaching an agreement with each other, and the law solves the collective action problem in large part by making it easier for parties to bargain with each other. The possibility that parties will be able to reach a bargain with each other in a reorganization that they could not have reached outside reduces the risk that creditors will end up in a place that is contrary to their collective interests. This in turn reduces the need for the judge to approve payments to prepetition creditors who are also active players in the case.

As the dynamics of reorganizations change, particular problems become more or less salient. One that became more important in recent years was that of dealing with a creditor who wears two different hats. Nothing requires creditors to have only one kind of claim against a firm. Recall, for example, that many participants in the AT&SF reorganization held both junior and senior bonds at the same time. It has become commonplace once again. Investors today trade actively and their positions in each tranche often change over time. These dynamics significantly complicate the task of overseeing the bargaining process. The vote of an investor who holds positions in multiple classes is not the same as the vote of an investor who holds only a single claim.

There is nothing inherently suspect about an investor buying into multiple parts of the capital structure. An investor may like the prices at which debt in multiple tranches is selling. Indeed, such a creditor may be more likely to think about the welfare of the firm as a whole because its investment spans the capital structure. As we saw with the AF&SF, having stakeholders with claims in multiple classes can bring benefits. A stakeholder with claims in multiple classes needs to worry less about whether creditors in one tranche are gaining an advantage at the expense of those in the other. For a creditor with positions in more than one tranche, the loss in one may lead to an offsetting gain in the other.

But holding claims in multiple classes requires additional scrutiny. When each creditor owns only one kind of stake in the debtor, those holding claims in a particular class should share similar goals. As they advance their own interests, they should also act in a way that advances the interests of others in their class given the rule that requires claims in the same class to be treated identically. This makes it easier to bind dissenters when unanimity is not possible. In the end, often the most sensible course is to trust the wisdom of crowds. If a supermajority thinks a plan is a good idea, it likely makes sense to bind someone who dissents. The voting rules work in part because the interests of everyone in the class are aligned.

A creditor who holds positions in two different tranches disrupts this mechanism. When the same investor holds claims in two classes, the investor's incentive is to vote to maximize the value of both claims. It will not focus on maximizing the value of its stake in one class to the exclusion of its stake in another. When the claims of such an investor are put in the same class as the claims of those invested only in that class, the interests of the stakeholders are no longer aligned.

Aladdin Hotel is a case that squarely faces the problem of investors wearing multiple hats.[35] It remains the starting place for those trying to make sense of this problem.[36] When it opened, in 1926, the Aladdin Hotel was the tallest building in Kansas City. The hotel was another grand project launched during the 1920s that encountered trouble during the Great Depression.

The Joneses, the owners of the hotel's equity, gained a controlling interest in its bonds as well. The bond indenture allowed a two-thirds majority to extend the date on which the principal was due. The Joneses sought to use their controlling interest in the bonds to push back their maturity date for ten years. The minority bondholders objected. They claimed that the Joneses were looking out for their interests as shareholders when they cast their bondholder vote. By postponing the maturity of the bonds, the Joneses benefitted themselves as

---

[35] Aladdin Hotel Co. v. Bloom, 200 F.2d 627 (8th Cir. 1953).

[36] This case has long been a focal point for thinking about how to regulate the rights of investors holding positions in multiple classes in a reorganization. (It figures prominently, for example, in the debates that led up to the adoption of the Bankruptcy Code.) The case itself, however, is a fight between bondholders outside of any collective proceeding.

shareholders. As such, the minority bondholders argued, the Joneses's vote to extend the maturity of the bonds was suspect. The court, however, rejected this characterization: "We have searched the record with great care and find no substantial evidence warranting a finding of bad faith, fraud, corruption or conspiracy of the Joneses."[37]

To be sure, when the Joneses voted, they took into account their interests as equityholders as well as their interests as bondholders, but the court found that the Joneses were not engaged in advantage-taking. Their intent was not to divert value from the other bondholders to themselves. Instead, the court believed, they were trying to maximize the value of the business.

Aladdin Hotel can be read to hold that although a stakeholder who wears two hats does not get a pass card, there is not a per se prohibition on being able to vote in both classes either. Instead, the judge should conduct a general inquiry into the reasonableness of that stakeholder's behavior. If the judge believes that the stakeholder is trying to maximize the value of the assets and is genuinely looking out for the interests of the firm as a whole, then the stakeholder's vote will count.

Some judges believe that the unwritten law leaves creditors wearing two hats under fewer constraints than *Aladdin Hotel* suggests. Under this view, stakeholders are allowed to maximize the value of their stakes in the firm, even if the actions they take benefit one stake they hold in the debtor at the expense of another. Creditors do not have to think about what is best for the firm as a whole. They just have to maximize their stake in the firm apart from their other interests. Whether this view is sound as applied to a large corporate reorganization, however, is not certain. There are cases in which courts approve of such behavior, but they typically arise in cases where the dynamics are strikingly different.

These cases are real estate cases like *Pine Gate*. The owner of a large rental apartment development encounters financial distress. It has one senior creditor that it owes $20 million and a handful of junior creditors owed just a few hundred dollars. The largest junior debt, amounting to just more than a third of all junior debt, is owed to an accountant, who is owed $100 for doing the books last week. (Because a management

---

[37] 200 F.2d at 631.

company typically runs the apartment building and pays itself out of the rents it collects, the debtor does not bear the operating expenses of the building itself.)

The debtor proposes a plan in which it would gradually convert the rental apartments into condominiums. The bank would be paid an amount equal to the value of its secured claim. The general creditors are paid almost 100 cents on the dollar in cash, and the equity-holders retain their stake. If the conversion succeeds, the equity-holders will benefit enormously. If the conversion fails, the senior creditor will bear the entire downside. It will have to spend years trying to sort out the mess of an unsuccessful property that is half rental and half condo.

The senior creditor approaches the accountant, buys the $100 claim for $100 in cash, and casts this vote against the plan. The senior creditor controls all the votes of the class of senior claims and more than a third of the votes of the unsecured class. By controlling both classes, the senior creditor ensures that no plan of the debtor can ever be confirmed.[38] If its vote of the accountant's claim is upheld, the court will be forced to dismiss the case. The senior creditor will foreclose, and there will be no payout at all to junior creditors.

The senior creditor's vote of the accountant's claim, of course, has nothing to do with its interests as a holder of this claim and everything to do with protecting its position as a senior creditor. The senior creditor and other members of the class of general creditors do not have interests that are aligned in any meaningful way. The senior creditor is opposing a plan that would pay the claims of general creditors nearly in full. By voting against the plan, the senior creditor is rendering its own junior claim worthless, as well as the claims of the other junior creditors. Allowing this lender to vote its junior claim in this fashion leaves the holders of general claims unequivocally worse off.

Nevertheless, judges in such cases have generally allowed the senior creditors to take control of the class of junior claims and exercise their votes in this fashion. One should be cautious about drawing larger lessons from these real estate cases. They are, in the end, examples of rough justice. Allowing the senior creditor to speak for the junior

---

[38] To confirm a plan, the debtor needs at least one class to accept it.

creditors is arguably justified because it makes little sense to give voice to these junior creditors in the first place. The junior claims are rounding errors.

Judges likely tolerate the senior creditor's vote of its junior claims because they are reluctant to confirm a plan that only a handful of junior creditors owed a trivial amount of money support. The claim of a small-time accountant and a few other service providers should not decide whether a multi-million-dollar apartment building should become a condominium. This concern does not arise in complicated reorganizations in which strategic investors wear multiple hats. They are different situations entirely. Similarly, if an investor holds positions both as a creditor and a shareholder, courts will scrutinize the actions especially closely. With insider status comes control and a heightened risk of special dealing.

It might seem sensible to minimize the two-hat problem when a non-insider holds different types of debt by allowing those who wear only one hat to insist on being in their own class if they want, but not allowing those with two hats to insist on being classified apart. This rule at least has the advantage of not giving a creditor the unilateral ability to create its own class by buying a claim in another class. But even allowing the one-hat creditors to insist on separate classification still creates fragmentation and makes confirmation harder merely because another creditor is wearing two hats.

There are other approaches to the two-hat problem. One approach, of course, is the middle position of *Aladdin Hotel*. A creditor holding positions in multiple classes can cast votes in each, but the court will scrutinize each vote to ensure that it is cast in good faith. Another is an approach Congress considered but explicitly rejected when it passed the 1978 Bankruptcy Reform Act. Under this approach, a creditor can vote in only one class. One more approach is to follow the paradigm of real estate cases. Creditors with positions in multiple classes can maximize their stake in the firm even when their interests are not aligned with other members of the same class.

The court in *Adelphia* adopted this approach.[39] *Adelphia* involved a more complicated two-hat problem than *Aladdin Hotel*. It involved

---

[39] In re Adelphia Communications Corp., 359 B.R. 54 (Bankr. S.D.N.Y. 2006).

a reorganization of a corporate group. There was one economic firm but multiple corporate entities. One creditor held a substantial stake in one class of the parent's debt and a controlling stake in one class of the subsidiary's debt as well. Increasing the value of one came at the expense of the other. A group of creditors who held interests in only one class objected that the creditor that wore two hats used its power to vote in their class to force through a plan that disproportionately favored its stake in another class.

The court in *Adelphia* allowed the vote to stand. The judge showed no particular sympathy for the creditor. Quite the contrary. The judge was plainly annoyed with the way this creditor had conducted itself during the negotiations. But this was neither here nor there. The judge began with the idea that the presence of creditors with positions in multiple classes was inevitable in large cases. As long as insiders were not involved and as long as those involved were merely advancing their own position as creditors (even if as a holder of a claim in another class of a related debtor), they were free to vote however they wanted.

The judge was merely the referee to ensure that the plan formally complied with the requirements of the Bankruptcy Code. Beyond that, it was up to the parties to forge their own bargain. Distressed debt investors are like those who found themselves in a knife fight in the Wild West. The judge put it this way:

> To be sure, a culture has developed ... in which many consider it acceptable, and indeed expected, to use the litigation process as a means to assert or follow through on threats. ... But aside from saying ... that I don't like such tactics and that they are a good way to irritate the judge, I don't think that I can or should do anything about them.[40]

This judge's understanding of first principles illustrates how the judges understand their role. They must ensure the playing field is level. Any plan must meet the substantive standards laid out in the statute. These include requirements that similarly situated creditors can insist on being treated the same way, and that classes of senior creditors can insist on absolute priority. But everyone is a sophisticated professional. When they bargain with one another, they have to look out for their own

[40] 359 B.R. at 63.

interests. The judge does not tell them the kind of deal they must reach. The judge merely ensures that no one acts in a way that is underhanded. As long as they are seeking to maximize the value of their stakes in the business, they are allowed to engage in brinkmanship and heavy-handed negotiating. One hopes that cooler heads will prevail, and parties will reach a deal. But if they do not, it is not for the judge to protect them.

The waters become murkier when, instead of a creditor buying claims in another class, a third party enters and is doing something other than maximizing the value of its claim. The same judge in *Adelphia* confronted what might seem a similar conflict between someone who held both a claim in one tranche of debt and a derivative instrument in another. He found the situation altogether different.[41] A hypothetical can lay out the problem and show why this problem is not the same.

Assume there is ParentCo and its wholly owned subsidiary, SubsidiaryCo. ParentCo has only one class of debt. The investor holds a blocking vote in this class. No plan can be confirmed without its affirmative vote. Then there is SubsidiaryCo. It again has a single class of debt. The investor holds no debt in SubsidiaryCo, but instead has taken a short position in it.

SubsidiaryCo owes money to ParentCo, but there is a dispute about how much. A plan is proposed that includes a settlement of the dispute with SubsidiaryCo, but the investor does not believe that ParentCo is receiving as much as it should from SubsidiaryCo. The investor votes its claims in the parent against the plan. It wants ParentCo to press for a better settlement with SubsidiaryCo. Other creditors of ParentCo disagree.

The investor's behavior may not seem so bad. A higher settlement from SubsidiaryCo makes the other creditors of ParentCo better off. The investor is also not taking a position that is inconsistent with its economic stake in ParentCo. It is pushing for a settlement that will increase the value of its stake in ParentCo. How hard ParentCo should push is the kind of judgment that each investor must make, and judges are poorly equipped to second-guess such decisions. In contrast to the

---

[41] In re DBSD, Inc., 421 B.R. 133, 143 (Bankr. S.D.N.Y. 2009) aff'd, 2010 WL 1223109 (S.D.N.Y. Mar. 24, 2010), aff'd in part, rev'd in part, 627 F.3d 496 (2d Cir. 2010).

other creditors with claims against ParentCo, however, this investor also stands to benefit from its short position if ParentCo can improve on the terms of the settlement. The more SubsidiaryCo has to pay, the less it will be worth and the more valuable the investor's short position.

The investor's short position is pulling in the same direction as its position in the capital structure. But other creditors of ParentCo do not gain quite as much as the investor if a more favorable settlement is achieved. The investor makes money from a bigger settlement in two ways, not just one. Every dollar that SubsidiaryCo pays to ParentCo decreases the value of its debt and correspondingly increases the value of the short position. As a result, the investor is going to be tougher in negotiations. It is more willing to risk bargaining failure than the other creditors of ParentCo because it has more to gain from holding out.

The difference between holding a short position and wearing a second hat might seem of little moment. They both put an investor in a position different from that of others in its class. But there is a difference, and it is critical. Today's judges exercise their policing powers narrowly. For the most part, they allow parties to pursue their own interests in the debtor, but they do insist that everyone focuses *on the debtor*. Maximizing such a stake is not what is happening when the investor is also trying to maximize the value of a short position. A short position does not reflect a contribution of capital in the firm. Reorganization law focuses on maximizing the value of the estate. It can insist that players focus on this when they cast their votes on a plan and not on their interests in other ventures, including short positions or, to say the same thing, side bets.

Reorganization professionals have long developed their own customs and practices. When these lead to an agreement that enjoys universal support, there is no action for the judge to take, even if the written law stands in tension with the custom. It is more complicated, however, when these same customs and practices lead to a plan that enjoys broad consensus, but a few dissenters, like the ones in *Los Angeles Lumber*, raise objections if only to promote their own agendas.

The more the norms of professionals drift away from their statutory moorings, the harder it becomes for judges to exercise oversight. Judges want professionals to reach a bargain through a process that is even-handed but knowing exactly what such a process looks like becomes hard when the parties themselves have the ability to introduce new patterns and practices that have the effect of changing the rulebook. The next chapter turns to this challenge.

8 LOOKING FOR RUNWAY

At the core of contemporary reorganization law are the same principles that animated the law at the time of Robert Morris, and the law remains under the spell cast by William O. Douglas, Jerome Frank, and other New Deal reformers. At the same time, today's judges understand that their mandate is narrow and that their ambitions must be modest. They must bring the parties together and ensure that the rights of all the stakeholders are protected at the same time. Bargaining that fails to include everyone is suspect. Disclosure is the order of the day. Parties do not have to behave altruistically, but they cannot pursue outside agendas. And if they deliberately throw sand into the gears of the reorganization, they can find their claims subordinated or even disallowed. At the same time, however, judges are not themselves equipped to chart a new course for a distressed business, nor is it their responsibility to protect sophisticated professionals. Professionals can look out for their own interests. The firm belongs to them, not the judge, and they are the ones who must chart its destiny.

Part of each judge's job is to push the parties towards consensus, and how they go about doing this is left to their good judgment. One well-respected judge tells parties that while he stands ready to decide even existential questions according to the letter of the law, any settlement they reach among themselves will be better than the one he imposes on them. They can never be certain what he will do. They can insist he rules on the matter at hand, but they should know that when they do, they are entrusting their fate to a monkey with a gun. This speech usually leads parties to forget about their lines in the sand

and settle. And if it does not, the judge decides the issue as best he can and still sleeps comfortably at night. He gave them fair warning.

An extreme example of how far a judge might go to bring parties to an agreement took place towards the end of the bankruptcy of the stockbroker Drexel Burnham. The parties were deadlocked over how to divide a large pool of junk bonds. Weeks of negotiation had left them at an impasse. The judge brought the parties together and told them that, given their inability to agree upon a deal, he had resolved to order the sale of the assets, even though a sale of such highly illiquid assets would yield them relatively little. Their inability to reach agreement forced his hand. He announced that he had made up his mind. He was ready to sign the appropriate order then and there, but other judicial business required him to take a phone call in his chambers. He promised the parties that he would return within the hour to sign the order. He left the courtroom, and the parties, after months of deadlock, sat down to negotiate one last time. Just before the judge returned an hour later as he had promised, they reached an agreement. One of them memorialized it in long hand on a yellow legal pad, and everyone signed.[1]

When such efforts work and the parties reach unanimous agreement through an open process untainted by ulterior motives or side deals, there is little controversy. That a deal was struck itself is the measure of success. Matters become more complicated, however, when an agreement wins broad support, but support is not unanimous. It is even harder when the agreement appears to stand in tension with an explicit statutory command.

In *Marvel Entertainment*, for example, the court approved the debtor's plan to continue shipping product for which customers had already paid even though prepaying buyers are ordinary general creditors who in the statutory distribution scheme are supposed to share pari passu with all the general creditors. In this case, the cost of shipping was small, and the production costs were largely sunk. More to the point, a failure to ship would sow unhappiness in the customer base and a loss

---

[1] Nancy Miller, Judge Rules With Rod, Impish Smile, USA Today, March 25, 1992, at 5B. The lawyer who led the negotiations and wrote out the agreement kept the yellow sheet of paper and later framed it in his office.

of patronage in the future. The products in question were comic books, and the prepaying buyers were subscribers.

Apart from the sheer silliness of serving tens of thousands of twelve-year-olds with proper notice and inviting them to be heard as creditors in a large reorganization, demanding that the twelve-year-olds pay a second time for *Spiderman* and the *Fantastic Four* would undermine the future of the comic business. Stopping the shipment of products would save little money and would do considerable reputational damage. All the other stakeholders would be worse off if subscribers were treated like ordinary creditors. For these purposes, the twelve-year-olds were more sensibly treated as future customers rather than as prepetition creditors. What was valuable to the estate (the goodwill of the subscribers) was not something that the estate enjoyed as of right. The estate could continue to enjoy their goodwill only by servicing the subscriptions.

Such a decision, of course, stands in tension with the substantive right of each creditor to share pro rata in the estate. If objection were raised, the judge is ordinarily bound to anchor the authority to issue the order. There is a provision in the Bankruptcy Code that allows the judge to "issue any order, process, or judgment that is necessary or appropriate to carry out the provisions of this title."[2] This is, however, a weak reed, unless the judge can point to some specific substantive provision of the statute that the exercise of this power would vindicate.

In the case of shipping the comics, no single creditor is likely to raise an objection. It would be too likely to be seen as disruptive. Creditors do not want to identify themselves as troublemakers at the very start. The judge possesses many ways, large and small, to make that creditor's life miserable. Most experienced professionals understand better than to raise objections for their own sake. Judges rarely have to stare such a troublemaker down in open court and ask point blank, "Are you trying to blow up my case?" But they will do this if pressed. A judge will suspend the hearing, retire from the courtroom, and leave it to the other professionals to bring the miscreant back into line.

But sometimes proposals that make sense nevertheless stray too far from what the statute explicitly licenses. Some deals "alter the balance"

[2] Bankruptcy Code §105(a).

of substantive rights set out in the statute so much that they are not permissible.[3] The Supreme Court confronted such a case several years ago. A trucking firm went through a leveraged buyout two years before it tried to reorganize. When it entered Chapter 11, its sole asset was an action against the private equity fund that engineered the buyout. The action was not frivolous but was unlikely to yield much. No lawyer would take such an action on a contingent fee basis. As the judge overseeing the reorganization put it, any lawyer who took on such a case for a contingent fee "ought to have his head examined."

The private equity fund was willing give the estate something to settle the estate's cause of action against it, but there was a complication. One set of creditors, unpaid workers, had a completely independent cause of action against the same private equity fund, and they did not have the resources to bring it. They could bring claims against the private equity fund only if they received a large enough distribution from the debtor's bankruptcy. The private equity fund conditioned any settlement of the debtor's action against it on none of the distribution going to the workers. It was willing to give something to buy peace with the estate, but only if did not come at the cost of starting another war on a different front.

There was no commandeering or corruption of the process. The private equity firm was transparent about its motives in open court. As its lawyer explained to the judge, "[I]f the money goes to the [workers], then you're funding somebody who is suing you who otherwise doesn't have funds."[4] The opportunity to settle with the private equity fund belonged to the debtor and could be monetized only if the representatives of the debtor could strike a deal with the private equity fund.

When approached to make such a settlement with the debtor, the private equity fund was under no duty to the debtor. It was simply open to doing a deal that was in its self-interest. For its part, the debtor was seeking to trade one asset (a suspect fraudulent conveyance action that it could not afford to pursue) for another that was more valuable to it (the money the equity fund was willing to pay to make the action go away).

---

[3] See Czyzewski v. Jevic Holding Corp., 137 S. Ct. 973, 987 (2017).

[4] In re Jevic Holding Corp., 787 F.3d 173, 177 n.4 (3d Cir. 2015), rev'd and remanded sub nom. Czyzewski v. Jevic Holding Corp., 137 S. Ct. 973 (2017).

It did not seem that the creditors' committee was selling out workers. The deal did not hurt the workers. With or without the deal, the workers would recover nothing. The deal, however, did give cash to the other creditors, something they would not have without it. The transaction, as Justice Kagan characterized it during the oral argument, was Pareto superior, an economic term for a transaction that makes some better off without making anyone else worse off.

In theory, such value-maximizing transactions seem unproblematic even if they require cutting a deal with prepetition creditors or someone else with a history with the debtor. The creditors as a group were better off as was the equity fund. Mutually beneficial bargains are inherently desirable. Turning them down leaves money on the table.

Nevertheless, ruling some transactions out of bounds may bring benefits across the mine run of cases, even if some value-maximizing transactions in individual cases are lost in the process. In policing the process, the judge must take account of the potential for parties to engage in strategic behavior. The judge must also bear in mind the potential for error. Tying oneself to the mast is sometimes a good idea.

Cases in which maximizing the value of the estate actually requires proceeds from an otherwise beneficial transaction to be distributed at the end of the case contrary to the pro rata distribution rule (or indeed any other distributional rule) are rare. It is seldom that, holding its own share constant, one party affirmatively wants some of the other parties to receive more and others less. Rational economic actors care about their own welfare, not about how an arm's-length transaction affects the welfare of some other party. And even when such cases exist, many value-maximizing transactions can be salvaged through bargaining among the stakeholders.

One cannot exclude the possibility that Pareto superior transactions exist in which value will be lost unless assets are divided up at the end of the case in a way that departs from the scheme set out in the Bankruptcy Code. But the rarity of such cases favors a hard-line rule. Strictly enforcing distributional rules limits costly rent-seeking. A creditor who cannot receive more than its pro-rata share is disabled from bargaining for more. The estate, in most cases, is better off with fixed distributional rules especially when few, if any, cases actually require distributional flexibility.

As the Supreme Court held in *Boyd*, process is what matters. Courts do not dictate the terms of the plan, but all stakeholders must have an opportunity to participate in addition to being given a "fair offer." Shareholders cannot sell out and decline to exercise the vigilance that would have worked to the benefit of the general creditors as well as themselves. They cannot exclude the general creditors from the bargaining. Nor can they enter into a side deal that has the effect of compromising the general creditors' rights.

But it is hard to demarcate the exact limits of how much of the letter of the law must be applied in a world in which modern reorganization practice has a shape that is radically different from what those who refashioned the law in the 1970s anticipated. The norms of bankruptcy lawyers as they have evolved have side-lined a number of explicit statutory rules. Judges do not insist on enforcing them when the bargaining process itself is otherwise uncompromised and the objections are not substantial.

A few years ago, an eager and well-schooled young lawyer joined the restructuring group of one of the United States's preeminent law firms. On his first day at the firm, he was asked to attend a meeting where the final touches on a plan of reorganization were being put in place. His job, he was told, was to ensure that the indenture trustee, who had done nothing, was paid nothing.

The assignment was straightforward. Indenture trustees are the agents charged with representing the interests of bondholders. It was plain that this indenture trustee, like many, had been an idle bystander during the case, and the statute explicitly provides that indenture trustees are paid only if they make a "substantial contribution."[5] When the moment came to register his objection, the new lawyer, anxious to make his mark, confidently pointed to the statutory mandate and the compelling evidence that the indenture trustee had made no contribution. When he had finished, he confidently looked around for signs of assent, only to find that, far from quickly agreeing with him, the lawyers around the conference table were not taking him seriously. They gave him the distinct impression that what he had proposed was silly.

---

[5] Bankruptcy Code §503(b)(5).

One of the least important norms of modern reorganization professionals is that the fees of indenture trustees are always paid. Fighting over them is more trouble than it is worth. Only someone who is not part of this world would suggest otherwise. This is why the other lawyers were amused and why the partners at his firm gave this young lawyer the assignment in the first place. It was good fun. It was akin to asking a new apprentice in a French restaurant to retrieve soufflé weights lent to a rival.[6] And it reminded the lawyer that, however well he had been taught in law school, he still had much to learn.

The judge has little interest in policing the fees of indenture trustees in the face of such norms. In the grand scheme of things, they are small beer. But other modern practices present bigger challenges. Many arise because changes in the way various players approach the reorganization process unsettle long-time practices.

The boards that oversee public firms in deep financial distress no longer see their job as protecting the interests of the shareholders. Their duties go to the firm as a whole rather than to existing equityholders.[7] When a firm finds itself in financial distress, directors are judged by whether the firm reorganizes successfully, not by how ownership interests in the firm are divided among the stakeholders. They care most about ensuring that the firm emerges successfully and quickly from the reorganization. What keeps them up at night is the reputational hit they will take if the firm blows up on their watch.[8] What happens to the old shareholders or any other constituency is an afterthought.

---

[6] See, e.g., Jacques Pépin, The Apprentice: My Life in the Kitchen (Houghton Mifflin Harcourt 2003). There is, of course, no such thing as a soufflé weight.
   In recent years, the role of indenture trustees has changed somewhat. Nowadays, the bondholders will often organize themselves during a reorganization and replace the incumbent indenture trustee with a new trustee who will be responsive to the noteholders and more active in the reorganization case. Moreover, objections to the practice of paying indenture trustees in those cases in which they remain idle have started to come from the United States trustee. The United States trustee has been on a mission to eliminate any departures from the letter of the law, no matter how widely accepted they are. But judges do not pay much attention.
[7] See Quadrant Structured Products Co. v. Vertin, 102 A.3d 155 (Del. Ch. 2014).
[8] To be sure, board members of firms that are reorganizing may hold equity stakes in the business, but these are not likely to be a large part of their portfolios. Among other things, even a large equity stake is not worth much when the firm is in financial distress. And members of the board are not likely to be part of the business over the long haul. Most will be replaced in any reorganization.

This posture changes the way directors approach reorganizations. Critical to them is the enormous power that senior creditors now wield in large reorganizations. By the time the debtor encounters financial distress, and a reorganization is in prospect, its principal lender has usually taken a security interest in all of the debtor's assets and actively manages the debtor's cashflows through a revolving credit facility. All the cash coming into and leaving the business passes through this lender's hands. Modern technology enables the lender to know precisely how much cash its debtor has at any given time. By virtue of controlling the business's cashflows, the creditor is less dependent upon the debtor to tell it what is going on. The creditor has experience in the industry and thus can readily distinguish between cashflow problems related to a general industry downturn and such problems that are unique to its debtor and the debtor's management team.

Moreover, the debtor is likely to have tripped one of the covenants in the senior creditor's loans. The power to declare a default allows the senior creditor to begin negotiations about the future of the business. Once they decide a reorganization is needed, the senior creditor and the debtor will attempt to reach an understanding about financing the case. The two will also negotiate an agreement about the shape of the reorganization plan. This "restructuring support agreement" provides a template for the reorganization as it moves forward. The ability to craft such agreements and the willingness of courts to enforce them have decisively changed the dynamics of reorganization bargaining over the past decade.

Restructuring support agreements provide a base camp. Either before the reorganization or during it, the senior lender and the debtor agree on a timetable and the basic elements of a plan. Even if the details must be worked out and additional parties brought on board, the restructuring support agreement at least provides a point of departure. Restructuring support agreements provide conspicuous benefits, including a clearer, quicker, and more reliable path toward exit from the reorganization.

On the face of it, restructuring support agreements are a good thing. A reorganization is most likely to be successful if the managers and the major stakeholders have reached a general understanding about the path ahead of them. Restructuring support agreements ensure that everyone can be confident that the reorganization will proceed in a particular direction. Creditors do not want to back a plan unless they know the debtor will back it as well. For its part, the debtor wants to be sure that the creditors will keep their promise to vote for the plan and will place no hurdles in the way of its smooth adoption.

Restructuring support agreements often work in conjunction with the debtor-in-possession financing agreement. Senior creditors agree to provide debtor-in-possession financing or consent to cash collateral at the same time that they enter into restructuring support agreements. There can be cross-default clauses, such that a failure to meet a milestone under the restructuring support agreement is a default under the debtor-in-possession loan. Similarly, a failure of the debtor to comply with the conditions of the postpetition financing agreement can be a default under the restructuring support agreement. Such a default entitles the senior creditor to walk away from the plan that was on the table.

Restructuring support agreements, when entered into or modified after the start of the case, illustrate the extent to which the judge's commitment to overseeing effective negotiations stands in tension with explicit statutory directives. Once a debtor enters a reorganization, a provision of the Bankruptcy Code explicitly limits the ability of parties to strike deals with each other. It prohibits solicitation of "acceptance or rejection of a plan" before the court has approved a disclosure statement, a document like a prospectus in a securities offering. It describes the plan and allows each creditor to understand what will happen to its claim if it votes in favor of it.[9] This provision is a relic of the New Dealers' concern that courts overseeing reorganizations needed to prevent insiders from negotiating plans that benefited themselves at the expense of innocent outsiders. In the absence of adequate disclosure about the plan, unsophisticated outside investors will not know how to exercise their votes. With it, as with a prospectus, unsophisticated investors can learn where they stand.

Such a disclosure mandate, however, interferes with the ability of anyone to form a plan in a world in which claims are constantly trading hands. Obtaining informal, nonbinding assurances from a creditor to

---

[9] See Bankruptcy Code §1125.

support a particular plan does not violate the prohibition, but informal understandings and assurances such as these, however, are often not enough. The holder of a particular claim may be a bank one day and a vulture investor the next. To push the plan process forward, plan proponents want binding commitments. But this creates a problem. When a debtor negotiates with a particular creditor and exacts its binding promise to support a particular restructuring in this fashion, it might seem that the debtor has solicited the "acceptance" of a plan of reorganization. But for restructuring support agreements even to be permissible, this cannot be so.

Modern judges typically permit parties to make such agreements notwithstanding what seems to be the explicit prohibition against them in the Bankruptcy Code.[10] These judges point to clauses in the restructuring support agreements that give fiduciary outs to the parties, the existence of various termination events, and the fact that creditors cast their actual votes only after the disclosure statement is approved.

Much of this is handwaving. The unwritten obligation of the judge to oversee the negotiations in its modern form is at odds with a statutory mandate that is a relic from an earlier age. Judges must uneasily confront a reality in which many different constituencies are fluid, and such agreements are needed to make plans possible.

Many judges simply look the other way when it comes to enforcing this provision of the Bankruptcy Code. What matters most are that the players in large reorganizations are sophisticated, distressed debt investors who have little in common with the small, undiversified individual investor saving for retirement whom Frank and Douglas wanted to protect. Sometimes courts are willing to bless such agreements explicitly.[11] On other occasions, they tell

---

[10] See, e.g., In re The Heritage Org., LLC, 376 B.R. 783, 791 (Bankr. N.D. Tex. 2007) ("[I]f a creditor believes that it has sufficient information about the case and the available alternatives to jointly propose a Chapter 11 plan with another entity . . ., it is absurd to think that the signing of a term sheet by those parties . . . is an improper solicitation of votes in accordance with §1125(b)."); In re Indianapolis Downs, LLC, 486 B.R. 286, 296 (Bankr. D. Del. 2013).

[11] In In re Residential Capital, LLC, 2013 WL 3286198 (Bankr. S.D.N.Y. 2013), the court approved the debtor's entering the plan support agreement and also found that each of the parties to the agreement acted reasonably and in good faith.

professionals concerned about the statutory prohibition informally just not to worry about it.[12]

Restructuring support agreements illustrate how judges police new practices using principles that existed in the earliest days of the republic and that have evolved continuously ever since. Courts are most likely to approve a support agreement when the agreement puts the debtor on a clear path toward reorganization. On the other hand, they will use their powers to strike down a support agreement, regardless of when it was reached, that merely enables one creditor to acquire a commanding position in the case in return for offering a benefit that inures to the debtor or its managers rather than the creditors as a group.[13] They strike down such agreements not because they violate any statutory command, but because they are at odds with longstanding principles, at least as those principles are now understood.

In addition to deciding whether to recognize reorganization support agreements, the judge must account for the way that they change the dynamics of the negotiations. The support agreement has evolved well beyond a straightforward document that sets out the substance of the plan that the parties intend to put before the court. It also sets out the process for getting it confirmed. The typical support agreement contains a number of milestones. The final debtor-in-possession financing order and the disclosure statement must be approved by a specified date. Deadlines are similarly fixed for voting and plan confirmation.

By signing the restructuring support agreement, the debtor commits itself not only to particular substantive terms in a plan, but also to a way of conducting itself during the reorganization. The debtor promises not to bring any avoidance actions against parties to the agreement. It promises to oppose the appointment of a trustee or an examiner with expanded powers. The appointment of an equity committee terminates the support agreement.

---

[12] One lawyer reported that his concerns about restructuring support agreements were once brushed aside from not one, but two judges simultaneously as he was about to walk into a mediation session with them in which such an agreement was to be negotiated. Being reassured in this fashion is not quite the same thing as having a judge formally approve them, but it usually suffices.

[13] See, e.g., In re Innkeepers USA Trust, 442 Bankr. 227 (Bankr. S.D.N.Y. 2010).

In one case, for example, the restructuring support agreement set out a number of triggering events, the effect of which was to oblige the debtor to reject collective bargaining and retiree obligations under a prescribed timetable.[14] If the debtor proved unable to renegotiate the collective bargaining agreements, the debtor was required to abandon the reorganization and pursue instead a going-concern sale. This mast-tying strategy limited the debtor's ability to give ground to the union and the retirees in the negotiations. Such agreements may go too far. The debtor has a statutory duty to negotiate in good faith with respect to collective bargaining agreements. Committing itself in advance in this fashion may be inconsistent with this duty, and the judge may forbid such provisions.

Restructuring support agreements are subject to frequent amendment and modification. But their importance should not be underestimated, even when there is no overt overreaching. These agreements start a ball rolling that is hard to stop. Once the debtor has committed itself to a restructuring support agreement with some creditors, the nonparticipating creditors find themselves in a difficult position. There is now less they can do to shape the plan in a way that advances their own interests. The plan laid out in the restructuring support agreement sets the agenda for the bargaining that follows. Here, as elsewhere, the ability to set the agenda affects the terms of the final bargain.

A senior creditor can obtain a restructuring support agreement that gives it the ability to capture a comparatively larger share of the reorganization pie because those representing the debtor are not inclined to push back. Instead, they are focused on whether the restructuring support agreement, regardless of how it divides the spoils, is likely to lead to a confirmed plan. The restructuring support agreement provides the glide path for a smooth landing. If the price is a somewhat larger share of the reorganized business for the senior creditors, it is a price they are happy to pay. They are searching for runway.

Once the debtor and the senior lender enter a restructuring support agreement, successive ones follow. The debtor is likely to turn next to the one among the more junior creditors who can do the most to ensure

---

[14] Walter Energy Restructuring Support Agreement §11(g) & (h); Motion for an Order Authorizing the Debtors to Assume a Restructuring Support Agreement at 112–14, In re Walter Industries, Inc., No. 15–02741 (Bankr. N.D. Ala. July 15, 2015) ECF No. 44.

that the firm reorganizes successfully. The deal struck with this creditor will ensure it does better than those who come later. Creditors who do not join such agreements are, in principle, entitled to insist on their substantive rights during the plan confirmation hearing, but they may find that they are left with relatively little. Because their priority rights cannot be defined with precision, it is easy for those in control to leave them shortchanged.

The new dynamic in reorganization practice recalls Louisiana governor Huey Long's appeal to prospective backers: "Those of you who come in with me now will receive a big piece of the pie. Those of you who delay, and commit yourselves later, will receive a smaller piece of pie. Those of you who don't come in at all will receive – Good Government!"[15] From the perspective of those who are not part of the restructuring support agreement, the theoretical ability to vindicate their substantive rights at confirmation is the equivalent of enjoying "good government."

A restructuring support agreement was put forward in one case several years ago that rewarded creditors who joined it with a "forbearance fee." This fee was funded by its nondebtor parent.[16] A critical provision of this restructuring support agreement called for those joining it to instruct their indenture trustee to forbear from pursuing separate actions against the parent. Because the agent was obliged to follow instructions by a majority, the deal, if it went into effect, would bind all the creditors. Such a deal might not have been possible outside of bankruptcy.[17] Nor could it be implemented in a reorganization plan, as those in the class who consented received something (the forbearance fee) that those who refused to join the agreement did not.

All of this suggests that judges should scrutinize such agreements with great care. It should make no difference that the money did not come from the estate. The critical question for the judge should be

---

[15] For one of many accounts of this episode, see Christopher Hitchens, *No One Left to Lie To: The Triangulations of William Jefferson Clinton* 17 (Verso 1999).

[16] See Caesars Entertainment Corp., Form 8-K, filed on July 21, 2015, at Item 1.01.

[17] The Trust Indenture Act limits the ability of parties to impose changes in major terms of a bond over the objection of any bondholder. Its reach, however, remains unclear. See Marblegate Asset Management LLC v. Education Management Finance Corp., 846 F.3d 1 (2d Cir. 2017).

whether such an agreement undermines the bargaining process. The judge needs to ask, for example, whether the forbearance fee is being used to hijack the process to protect a third party from litigation. If it is, the judge has the power to stop it.

Seen through this lens, the vices of restructuring support agreements are subtle. The most obvious consequence of using restructuring support agreements is that they leave creditors who have the greatest ability to put the reorganization off course with more and creditors who lack such power with relatively less. But it is not obvious that blessing a bargaining process in which senior creditors will receive more and junior creditors less should trouble us greatly. A mechanism that has the effect of rewarding those who come to agreement quickly could be seen as a good thing.

The ability to reorganize a firm more quickly and more cheaply may matter more than the way in which stakes in the reorganized firm are parceled out. And it is important to bear in mind that, even after deals are struck, the plan still has to be confirmable. The distortions of the distributions cannot be so great as to fall outside a certain range. The judge still has to find that the plan is consistent with the substantive provisions of the statute.

A restructuring support agreement may shift value to the senior creditors, but what matters most with distributional rules are not so much that they bring about any particular distribution, but rather that they facilitate bargaining. It might be a good thing if restructuring support agreements make it easier for parties to reach agreement. Some creditors, of course, will receive more and others less from restructuring support agreements than they would in a world without them, but sophisticated creditors should be able to account for such effects and ensure that they still enjoy the market return on their capital.

To be sure, such shifts in distributions between senior and junior creditors may lead to indirect efficiency losses. Giving some creditors more and others less may make capital in the aggregate more costly and harder to obtain. But showing that these losses are large enough to care about is hard. If the distributions themselves are not problematic, what exactly should the judge police? Perhaps the largest concern is whether the restructuring support agreement prevents the judge from being able to police the negotiations effectively. When a party agrees to support an agreement, information that the party might have provided to the judge will be lost unless it is coming from some other source. If a restructuring support agreement keeps the judge from being on top of the facts, it is suspect.

In ordinary two-party litigation, suppression of information by litigants is rarely a problem. A judge can reach the optimal outcome because there are liberal discovery rules, and each litigant has an incentive to reveal what the other hides. The situation is more complicated when there are multiple parties and only some of them have access to the relevant information. Often, relevant information, such as information that shows how much the firm is worth, is not readily discoverable, and individual creditors may lack the incentive to ferret it out. A restructuring support agreement may have the effect of silencing the person most likely to disclose the relevant information. Indeed, the deal may have been struck just for this purpose. A restructuring agreement might prevent a long and wasteful hearing that leads nowhere, but it might also short-circuit an inquiry into whether a senior creditor was in fact entitled to its priority position.

A restructuring support agreement might both move the case forward and silence someone who might have been a zealous advocate for others who are not in the courtroom and who need protection. The judge must assess the trade-off between getting the information and keeping the case on track. Judges are skeptical recipients of knowledge. They can draw inferences from what they are told, how they are told, and what they are not told.

Boyd's enduring lesson in this environment is that judges should use their oversight power to ensure that enough information flows to them. A plan is not "fair and equitable" if it keeps a judge in the dark, even if the substantive terms of the plan itself seem unobjectionable. And this idea applies more generally. A sale or any other disposition must also be done with everyone's cards on the table.

The judge does not assess the terms of any bargain struck as long as the bargain itself is within the parameters set out in the statute. But the lessons of the New Deal are not entirely lost. In policing restructuring support agreements, as with everything else in the reorganization, judges must still ensure that the process does not slight the rights of passive investors who lack access to information or the means to vigorously protect their interests.

In a large case several years ago, there were notes held by a number of creditors with rights to the same collateral and the same payment terms, but some had a higher interest rate and later due date. There was a dispute over whether the acceleration brought about by the reorganization obliged the debtor to pay a premium (called a "make-whole payment") on the notes. The amount of the make-whole payment, if it were owing, would be much more for those who had the notes with the higher rate of interest and later due date.

The debtor and a group of creditors that consisted mostly of the noteholders with the lower interest rate entered into an elaborate restructuring support agreement. Among its terms was an undertaking by the debtor to make a tender offer to all those holding first-lien debt for a fixed price. Nearly all noteholders with the lower interest rate accepted the tender offer, but only a third of those with the higher interest rate did.

On the face of it, this tender offer did not affect the rights of any who chose not to participate. The creditors who did not accept the tender offer had exactly the same substantive rights after the tender offer as before. If the nonassenting noteholders wanted to argue that they were entitled to make-whole payments, nothing in the restructuring support agreement prevented it. They might end up with less than under the tender offer if they litigated and lost, but in this respect they were no different than any other creditor who is given an offer to settle a claim and chooses to turn it down.

That the settlement took the form of a tender offer or was embedded in the restructuring support agreement had no effect on the substantive rights of the parties. All the creditors had a chance to accept the offer or take their chances. Indeed, in one sense the offer left nonassenting creditors better off. Because those who settled with the debtor were out of the picture, the nonassenting creditors would later find it easier to gather the necessary votes to reject the plan and force a full-scale hearing in which the judge would have to rule on the question of whether the make-whole was owed as well as the value of both the firm and the securities issued under the plan.

Such a tender offer would be problematic, however, if it short-circuited bargaining. For example, those holding the notes with the lower rate of interest might be concentrated among a few extremely sophisticated and litigious hedge funds. The rest might be widely dispersed among relatively remote investors. Assume the debtor and these hedge funds enter into the restructuring support agreement. The hedge funds accept the tender offer and comparatively few of the dispersed investors do.

It might seem that the dispersed investors have only themselves to blame. The outsiders who were not part of the agreement received the same offer for their notes as the insiders. But it is not this easy. Outside investors operate in a vacuum, and this allows for advantage-taking. The outside investors were forced to decide whether to tender before there was a disclosure statement. Indeed, the noteholders had to make their decision before the debtor even filed its schedules. If the debtor had been unable to make this offer, the hedge funds would have remained in the case and aggressively pushed the debtor to honor the make-whole provision. After the tender offer, the comparatively unorganized outsiders can no longer free-ride on these efforts.

The written law is silent about whether such tender offers are permissible. This is a domain in which the judge must rely on general principles. If many of the noteholders were indeed dispersed, the judge should have refused to allow the tender offer to go forward. It was not enough that such creditors would have the theoretical right to complain. An abiding legacy of William O. Douglas is that any deals cut in a reorganization cannot undermine the forces that provide meaningful protection to outsiders. The hedge funds should not be able to cut a deal that leaves them with extra money in their pocket any more than the two preferred shareholders in *Young v. Higbee*.

As it happened, however, those who chose not to tender in this case were actively involved in the case and fully informed.[18] There was no reason to think that the tender offer deterred anyone from making and aggressively pursuing every objection available to them. It made sense for the judge in that case to allow this unusual tender offer to go forward.

---

[18] They were sufficiently organized that they pursued the matter to the Third Circuit, where they were represented by Ropes and Gray, a storied global law firm founded in 1865 by Harvard law professor John Chipman Gray.

When exercising oversight, the judge needs to apply principles with an awareness of the parties and the conflicts between them. If they are repeat players who live by the same set of shared norms, there is comparatively less need to interfere. The judge will become more vigilant if well-established norms are slighted. For example, it is understood among reorganization professionals that you never send a threatening letter or file an aggressive pleading without giving opposing counsel the courtesy of a telephone call first. When you stab someone in the reorganization arena, you stab them in the chest, not the back. The judge will not sanction a party for violating such a norm, but if such norms are being violated and the judge learns about these violations the judge will be curious to know what else might be infecting the dynamics of the negotiations. The judge will become more apt to ask questions and insist more strongly that square corners be cut.

With a restructuring support agreement as with other innovations, the relevant questions remain the same, informed by the same principles that have been evolving for more than two centuries. Parties cannot enter side deals that keep matters from being fully and fairly vetted before the judge. Nor can judges allow anyone to commandeer the process or pay someone to look the other way. Whenever this happens, the judge must intervene.

In the modern reorganization world, however, negotiations should ordinarily be given considerable slack when the gladiators enter into the arena on equal terms. The judge must resist the temptation to unmoor the "fair and equitable" principle and similar language from history and theory. When well-represented, well-informed parties compete on a level field, the judge allows them to play on. Interventions should come only when the dynamics of the negotiations fail to account for the interests of the various constituencies and the stakes are large enough to make the game worth the candle.

The same judge who gave a pass to the tender offer intervened in the same case to reshape the bargaining environment dramatically. The distressed business consisted of a large constellation of related corporate entities. Each member of the corporate group had its own assets and its own creditors. Moreover, each of these entities had substantial legal rights against the others. The judge insisted each have independent directors and hire its own professionals. Taking this step could not be done casually. Insisting that each legal entity find separate representation is costly, but when many billions are at stake more can be spent on a process that ensures that every voice is heard.

At the same time the judge intervened, however, the judge was not tilting in favor of resolving the disputes in one way or the other. By training and discipline, the judge does not care how the differences between competing parties are resolved. The judge polices the bargaining to ensure only that the process respects the rights of all the players. As long as the process is sound, the negotiations themselves are largely beyond the judge's mandate. It is the province of the professionals, the heirs of Victor Morawetz, Henry Hirshberg, and Ron Trost. Such matters are left to them and their norms and their rituals.

The law of corporate reorganizations works as well as it does because its practitioners, like its judges, enjoy a shared understanding of its past. Return to this case involving the negotiations among the professionals tasked with representing the members of the corporate group who needed to sort out rights to what amounted to hundreds of millions in intercorporate claims. The same young lawyer who had not understood the fees of the indenture trustee some years before found himself at the head of the bargaining table. At the start, one of the most senior lawyers at the table pointed the young lawyer to a technical issue. The young lawyer in turn responded with a dismissive, "And what would you know about the law?" Everyone laughed. It was a perfect icebreaker. The suggestion that the senior lawyer did not know the law was not made seriously. They were all insiders, and insiders knew that the senior lawyer who had raised this technical issue had, many decades before, been one of the two congressional staffers who had drafted the text of the Bankruptcy Code. Suggesting that this lawyer did not know reorganization law was a backhanded way of showing respect, at least in this world. Our young lawyer had become a member of the club. And the bargaining began.

AFTERWORD

During the 1980s, Thomas Jackson and I showed how reorganization law took nonbankruptcy rights as it found them. It limited itself to sorting out the collective action problem that existed when a corporate debtor lacked the assets to meet all its obligations in full. The challenge was one of sorting out nonbankruptcy entitlements, ensuring that assets were being put to their highest valued use, and at the same time requiring the debtor to play by the same rules as everyone else. Although this view of reorganization law does not seem especially controversial today, it led to much sturm and drang, most notably perhaps in the spirited, but consistently civil debates that I had with Elizabeth Warren during this period.

This book has taken a different tack. It turns from the challenge of recognizing nonbankruptcy entitlements in a reorganization to focus more squarely on the reorganization process itself. Rather than reviewing the explicit rules set out in various sections of the Bankruptcy Code, it unpacks the larger principles that underlie them. Although second nature to experienced reorganization lawyers and judges, they are largely inaccessible to those outside this world.

Over the years, it has been my great privilege to work with a large number of gifted individuals, and it is no accident that most of the ideas in this book are ones I have learned from them. Collaborations I have had with other scholars are the most visible evidence of my indebtedness. Hence, most manifest is the help I have enjoyed from Donald Bernstein, Tony Casey, Edward Morrison, Randy Picker, and most especially Robert Rasmussen.[1] They have also helped me with this manuscript.

In addition, my orbit has crossed with many extraordinary academics, including Barry Adler, Ken Ayotte, Vince Buccola, Jared Ellias, Emily Kadens, Bruce Markell, and George Triantis. They too have shaped my thinking. Two who deserve a special note of thanks are Richard Levin and David Skeel. In addition to sharing much of their wisdom with me over the years, they read the manuscript with care and provided many incisive comments.

Finally, a large number of extraordinary judges and practitioners have illuminated this terrain for me. To the extent this book has merit, the credit must go to these individuals and many more. This list is too long to enumerate, but among them have been Thomas Ambro, Shelley Chapman, Robert Drain, Frank Easterbrook, Robert Gerber, Barbara Houser, Ken Klee, the late Harvey Miller, Hal Novikoff, Brendan Shannon, Christopher Sontchi, and Jane Vris. I owe a special debt to J. Ronald Trost. Long before providing me with a wealth of material I have used in this book, he introduced me to the National Bankruptcy Conference and enabled me to participate in its work.

In the course of preparing this book, I have enjoyed the support of the Frank Greenberg Fund, the able assistance of three outstanding research assistants, Kurt Cronican, Ben Nickerson, and Spencer Parts, as well as Mary Becker and Lisa Cornish, my copyeditors.

---

[1] The ideas developed in this book took nascent form in my work with them and other work that drew on ideas developed with them. For the material in Chapters 2 and 4, especially important was Douglas G. Baird & Robert K. Rasmussen, The End of Bankruptcy, 55 Stan. L. Rev. 751 (2002), and Douglas G. Baird & Robert K. Rasmussen, Control Rights, Priority Rights, and the Conceptual Foundations of Corporate Reorganizations, 87 Va. L. Rev. 921 (2001). Chapter 5 builds on Douglas G. Baird, Priority Matters, 165 U. Penn. L. Rev. 785 (2017), while Chapter 6 relies heavily on Douglas G. Baird & Donald S. Bernstein, Absolute Priority, Valuation Uncertainty, and the Reorganization Bargain, 115 Yale L.J. 1930 (2006). Core ideas in Chapter 7 were developed in Douglas G. Baird, Anthony J. Casey, & Randal C. Picker, The Bankruptcy Partition, 166 U. Penn. L. Rev. 1675 (2018), and Chapter 8 draws on Douglas G. Baird & Robert K. Rasmussen, Antibankruptcy, 119 Yale L.J. 648 (2010), and Douglas G. Baird, Bankruptcy's Quiet Revolution, 91 Am. Bankr. L.J. 593 (2017).

INDEX

CPSIA information can be obtained
at www.ICGtesting.com
Printed in the USA
LVHW022259070522
718181LV00016B/1385